Charter School Leadership

Elements for School Success

Cameron Curry

ROWMAN & LITTLEFIELD EDUCATION
A division of
ROWMAN & LITTLEFIELD PUBLISHERS, INC.
Lanham • New York • Toronto • Plymouth, UK

Published by Rowman & Littlefield Education
A division of Rowman & Littlefield Publishers, Inc.
A wholly owned subsidiary of The Rowman & Littlefield Publishing Group, Inc.
4501 Forbes Boulevard, Suite 200, Lanham, Maryland 20706
www.rowman.com

10 Thornbury Road, Plymouth PL6 7PP, United Kingdom

British Library Cataloguing in Publication Information Available

Library of Congress Cataloging-in-Publication Data

Library of Congress Cataloging-in-Publication Data Available

ISBN 978-1-4758-0326-6 (cloth : alk. paper)—ISBN 978-1-4758-0327-3 (pbk.   )—ISBN
978-1-4758-0328-0 (electronic)

Printed in the United States of America

Table of Contents

Acknowledgments

To Barbara for your unwavering love, support, and encouragement that gave this flight wings.

For Jordan, Elizabeth, and Kate to know that all things are possible.

To John and Kevin for always believing.

To Ashley for your attention to detail and editing that brought the extra shine.

To Rebecca for your guidance, candor, encouragement, and push that I needed to start this journey.

This book is for the dreamers and believers: for the ones who want to make a difference for students and communities, in pursuit of improving public education for us all.

Preface

"Are you bored with life? Then throw yourself into some work you believe in with all your heart, live for it, die for it, and you will find happiness that you had thought could never be yours." —Dale Carnegie, American writer

We have heard it said a thousand times, "If you have nothing nice to say, don't say anything at all!" If one were to make a small change to this age-old statement of wisdom, it could be related to leadership: "If you have nothing of *value* to say, don't say anything at all."

We have all found ourselves at a dinner party, a meeting, or surrounded by strangers when the conversation is moving at a good clip, wondering what to say or when to leap into the stream of dialogue without missing a beat. The goal is to add some significance based on our point of view, while contributing some meaningful value to the interaction.

I know a few people—and I am sure you also have these people in your life—who can pontificate way too long on subjects they know little or next to nothing about. These individuals tend to be the resident expert that can clear a room, or send the party packing! The rest of the guests would love to get a word in edgewise and enjoy the free-flow of information and ideas, but they are halted by the know-it-all who is stealing the conversation. We often want to avoid these individuals, and we certainly don't want to be known as one!

These are among the thoughts that I considered after 13 years in charter school education. Did I have something significant to add to today's educational conversation? If so, what? As a business and educational leader, I know how much I value spending a few minutes, hours, or days with someone who has run the race before me. What that professional has to share will help me avoid missteps, allow me to see the current "forest for the trees," and encourage me to make better decisions based on his or her experiences.

My desire in writing this book was not to be the loudmouth at the dinner party but rather the colleague, friend, or mentor who can offer you words of encouragement and sound advice about how to create, grow, and manage a thriving public charter school.

So in sharing a bit of entrepreneurial wisdom with you, my first piece of advice would be to learn whom to listen to, whose experience can be valuable and gleaned from, and how and when to apply this knowledge to your particular circumstances. I plan to share from my past professional experience of failures and successes since launching my charter school leadership career in 1999 by working in a start-up public charter school that has become a thriving and successful educational organization.

In California, the Charter Schools Act of 1992 opened the door for innovation in public schools that embraced parent choice. The tapestry of my past work experience was clearly woven with appreciation, passion, and the fortitude to survive the wild ride of creating, growing, and managing a new nonprofit public charter school of choice known as The Classical Academies, where I serve as the executive director.

In 1999, our challenges were swift and steep. We needed to find facilities, hire a team, and locate furniture and fixtures—all in the faithful pursuit of opening a school to serve elementary students, kindergarten through eighth grade. Being a new charter school, with limited resources, added another layer of challenges as the deadline to open our doors preceeded the state's timeline in sending pupil funding to cover the costs of operation.

Over the past decade, I have seen one kindergarten through eighth grade elementary school with 220 students grow into three award-winning public charter schools. These schools serve more than 2,600 students, train and empower more than 1,600 parents, and inspire and motivate more than 200 employees to be and to do their very best in service to others.

This combination of students, parents, and educators working collaboratively in an academic partnership has brought accolades and praise to our schools as well. Here are a few of these honors:

- Coastal Academy: First charter school in the state of California to receive recognition as being an Exemplary Independent Study Program.
- The Classical Academy: Second charter school in the State of California to receive recognition as being an Exemplary Independent Study Program.
- Classical Academy High School: Third charter school in the State of California to receive recognition as being an Exemplary Independent Study Program.
- Coastal Academy: Designated a California Distinguished School.
- Twelve straight years of exception-free financial compliance audits.
- All three schools received accreditation with the Western Association of Schools and Colleges (WASC).
- 96% satisfaction rating from parents with students in our program.
- Mid-800 Academic Performance Index (API) scores for all three schools.
- 2011 Hart Vision Award for Charter School Leader of the Year presented to Cameron Curry by the California Charter Schools Association.

- In 2012, Classical Academy High School was named a top high school in *Newsweek* magazine, *US News & World Report*, and the *Washington Post*.

What has allowed for the growth, development, and management of these successful public charter schools? I believe leadership is the key factor that has propelled our schools to reach new heights in providing exceptional customer service to families, stellar academic outcomes for students, and increased parent satisfaction with our programming.

My goal from the beginning has been to inspire my team with messages, reminders, and examples that detail:

- **Our Mission:** *Why are we in business?*
- **Our Culture:** *What is expected?*
- **Our Values:** *What is important, and why, as an organization?*

When empowered by this information, team members (a term I prefer to use over "staff") can effectively meet and exceed all expectations. At The Classical Academies, our employees are each grounded in our culture and understand the individual part they play that leads to the collective success of individual students and the organization. I will break down these concepts for you throughout the book so that you can readily apply them to your current and future leadership efforts.

I often utilize the idea of "crushing the pyramid" in my leadership work. The symbol of the pyramid is often the way many organizations run—from top to bottom. The peak of the pyramid is the leader of the organization, with the middle and wider base representing the layers of employees.

I prefer to view leadership as a playing field where team members are tasked with responsibilities, and then everyone shares the setbacks and successes knowing that we are all in this together. The synergistic response created when a team works together in this way helps propel the entire organization toward new successes. As you begin this next leadership adventure, envision what you hope your leadership will look like in the days ahead.

How do you want your organization to operate day in and day out?

Will you and your employees "crush the pyramid" and work together as a team?

In my experience, if you want to lead a successful charter school, you must also know the needs of your customers (students and parents), and then you must keep those needs aligned with your decision-making process. Maintaining customer satisfaction is paramount to a charter school's success. Happy parents (customers) will keep their students enrolled and your school in business.

There are many demands placed on charter school leaders, and among the most important are meeting the requirements of the state when it comes to student test results and accurate reporting on the school's finances. This is where a business-savvy school leader separates himself or herself from the rest.

Great school leaders must engage regularly in the daily operations and financial issues to keep a pulse on the backbone of the organization. Understanding the "business side" of operating a school is key for a leader to balance academic outcomes for students while managing the business of education within his or her organization.

I will address these essential aspects of charter school leadership so that your school can experience the kind of success that benefits students, parents, and the school community.

My desire in these pages ahead is to share what I have learned over the past 13 years in organizing, creating, and managing high-quality public charter schools. I have witnessed firsthand how small changes can make a substantial impact and how strategic thinking leads to improvement—academically and organizationally.

In my leadership work with my team, I focus on our schools' culture, mission, vision, communications, and encouragement. These five elements have led to increased job satisfaction and productivity of employees within the organization.

In the following chapters, I will break down these elements for you as part of our leadership conversation. I'll describe their importance, and I will share how you as a leader can embrace and use this information for the benefit of your school and community. Following each section, I will give you five key leadership points to remember.

Leadership matters. Your personal commitment to becoming a great charter school leader matters, too. Students, parents, and your community need your leadership. They are counting on you—so let's get started!

Introduction

"You cannot solve a problem with the same mind that created it!" —Albert Einstein, theoretical physicist

Some employees hold the perception that management is established to solve problems. Leadership is to meet with the employees who are causing those problems, and establish new rules to curtail any future difficulties that are coming next week, next month, or even next year. It just makes sense; leaders are the problem solvers and rule makers!

Funny thing is, once someone grants you access to the leadership chair your thinking quickly shifts. It has to. Leadership is really about establishing a workplace culture, creating a mission, articulating a vision, and exercising and utilizing great communications, while encouraging people to utilize good judgment in their day-to-day interactions for the betterment of all whom they serve.

Yet having to deal with problems also comes with the leadership territory. Let's be honest, if you label the daily distractions in leadership as "problems," you run the risk of being discouraged by the task at hand. Make the most of every situation and realize that leadership doesn't bring problems, but rather challenges and opportunities.

It is important to view challenges as opportunities to work with a team knowing that "all of us are smarter than some of us!" Leadership requires harnessing collaboration, communication, and commitment to reach a solution. The days of one individual providing all the insight, knowing all the answers, and being the keeper of the collective wisdom on what to do and when to do it are gone. Teams flourish when the leader involves members in leadership. Good leaders do it themselves. Great leaders involve others.

Sitting in the leadership chair is much harder than most people ever imagined that it would be. Leaders are ultimately responsible for their organization so they are often the receiver of the praises and the criticism. Unfortunately, they often garner more praise than they deserve, and often more criticism than they deserve. Many of us have worked under enough management styles to know when and if great leadership is in play.

Learning from experience, most know what is missing in ineffective managers so that when they get a chance in the leadership chair, they have a better idea of what to do and when to do it. Many individuals have had extensive training in "how *not* to lead," so just doing things differently from what they endured as an employee, by default, on most days, will be successful. Remember that it is easier to know what *not* to do than it is to know how to do it better. Just like parenting, effective leadership takes intuition, training, and practice.

Sound easy? It's not.

There is no one recipe that will produce a manager or leader who makes all the right decisions, or knows how to take the lead so that others will follow. If you have experienced great leadership, you have experienced the empowerment that comes as a result. A leader who plans, trains, and empowers his or her team will be a success.

All too often, employees are stuck with an unqualified manager who has never witnessed or seen real leadership functioning.

We have heard it said, "Leaders are born and not made!"

You may be one of those with a life and employment experience that begs to differ. It is my belief that strong leaders are born with common sense and good judgment. If you are a natural leader, your experiences, coupled with a strong mentor, can help shape you into a great manager who loves working with people.

These innate leaders can often be identified as children or young adults. They are the ones who organize their classmates and friends to play a game, or rally their peers to complete projects. When recognized, these hard-wired character traits can be molded appropriately.

There is no doubt that we all have gifts and abilities that can be nurtured to impact and influence others in the workplace. Someone who is decisive can make decisions, but in that same vein, that decisiveness can be seen as impulsive with short-term remedies, if those decisions only impact a few.

To be able to make good decisions requires seeking wise counsel, thinking things through to the end, and considering all of the ways your decision will impact others—in the short and long term.

A charter school leader needs to make decisions that support the entire organization, its growth, and its development. Leaders who delay, or who overanalyze a situation, can miss too many opportunities.

Timeliness and decisiveness go hand in hand with great leadership. Think about it. Purely from a business sense, did a leader like Donald Trump succeed by waiting days or weeks to make key real estate decisions? The easy answer is no. Mr. Trump is the picture of a decisive leader. He makes wise choices and never looks back with reservation.

So let's get specific.

Employees need to wrap their thoughts and actions around a company's mission, vision, and organizational culture. Their individual success is directly connected to their ability to follow, understand, and faithfully execute their roles within the organization based on these elements.

Individual employees need to understand that their actions impact the business' bottom line. A network of individuals understanding this translates into a team that can have a substantial impact on a community of students, parents, and professional educators.

What follows is a series of essential organizational elements that have led to the success of The Classical Academies and the students and parents whom we serve. The impact of leadership can be demonstrated through the use of messages that strengthen an employee's understanding of our mission, vision, and culture.

If leaders desire to be followed, they must manage their message and communicate in terms that connect with those whom they are leading.

If leaders fail in this effort, their rearview mirror will be filled with wide-open space instead of a thriving community of contributing employees who are passionately serving their charter school students, parents, and their community.

ONE

Enter the Culture Club

"Far and away the best prize that life offers is the chance to work hard at work worth doing." —President Theodore Roosevelt

A school culture can be defined as the actions, attitudes, and achievement standards a leader desires for a team to strive for in obtaining excellence within a community of learners.

Defining the workplace culture is critical to success in moving the workforce from ordinary to extraordinary. Employees thrive when they connect with a purpose, meaning, or cause that a leader has established.

When employees identify with those established culture elements, they are more likely to thrive and succeed where they are serving within the organization. They understand their role in the "big picture."

All groups of employees need leaders who clearly define the goals, objectives, and expectations if that organization has a desire to have a great and long-lasting impact. All too often leaders view the policies and procedures as the framework that creates a great organization. This is simply not true.

The framework of a great organization holds fast to the truth that valuing people is foundational to overall success. If a leader shifts that focus from people to process, the strength of that organization falters as the leader has moved away from the human element. A school's culture speaks to who a leader is, what he or she values, and what he or she plans to achieve.

School leaders who fail to implement a school culture fail to lead. In the void of leadership, chaos, mistrust, and a disconnect result. Employees find themselves rallying for change, leaving for change, or leading for change. The result is always the same in this case: change will happen with or without the leader's direction and influence.

1

Now the bigger question is, was this kind of planned and strategic change valuable and sustainable within the confines of the business, the school, or the industry?

Did the customers or parents find a safer, less chaotic, grounded learning community to educate their children in as a result?

When it comes to establishing and maintaining a great school culture, clearly defined actions, attitudes, and achievement standards that are valued will translate into creating a great school community.

Always remember, there is no such thing as small change.

How do you establish your organizational culture? What elements should you focus on as a school leader for your team to flourish and succeed?

Start with the basics.

ESSENTIAL CULTURE PROOF POINTS

What follows is the model incorporated within our school community that has led to connection, relevance, and sustainability for the team of educators at The Classical Academies.

This model has four elements of culture that our team has chosen to rally around. These culture points show our value for people who are passionate about making a positive impact, exercise good judgment, and connect and excel through effective communications.

Now let's define those culture points and unpack the value in each.

Culture Element 1: Employee Passion

The employee cares deeply about the mission. We have "the fire in the belly." We are intensely motivated to serve in our specific roles to benefit students, parents, and our fellow colleagues.

The employee is tenacious. We persevere in the face of difficult challenges, and we are tireless in search of new solutions. Do whatever it takes!

The employee will inspire others. We "rub off" on others in ways that make them willing to step up to new levels of commitment to our shared cause in pursuit of educational excellence.

The employee is selfless. We care deeply about the organization and set aside our self-interest. We do not worry about claiming credit for victories or assigning blame for setbacks.

The employee will bring heart. We recognize that the level of emotional commitment we have for our shared mission magnifies our strength. We value those who are open about their connection to the work because we know their example fuels our collective sense of purpose.

Employee passion is an essential element of success. Individuals who find enjoyment and fulfillment in their roles are more likely to excel and invest heavily in contributing to the organization's success.

Culture Element 2: Employee Making Positive Impact

The employee will accomplish incredible things. We complete an amazing amount of highly important work fully aligned with the strategic priorities of the organization.

The employee will follow through. We complete what we tell people we will accomplish.

The employee is results oriented. We focus on generating great results rather than always adhering to process. Procedures must always be evaluated and updated as necessary. We contribute solutions to obstacles.

The employee is biased toward action. We exhibit a clear preference for getting things done rather than analyzing excessively. When action is required and all angles and options are carefully considered, the best option will quickly surface. It may not be the perfect solution, but it will be a step in the right direction. Don't delay once the decision is made.

The employee has a desire to increase the impact of others. We value people who catalyze co-workers to greater competence. We take great pleasure in removing obstacles and releasing the potential of others.

Employees dedicated to making a positive impact are ones who value people over process. These team members keep the needs of others first and make an effort to see that success is achievable through their individual commitment to the organization.

Culture Element 3: Employee Utilizing Good Judgment

The employee does the right thing. We consistently make the right choice even when information might be incomplete or ambiguous.

The employee is intentional. We realize the organizational equivalent of intention is strategy. We constantly think strategically and can consistently articulate what we are doing, what we are *not* doing, and why we are doing it.

The employee prioritizes well. We are eager to learn about the organization's strategic priorities and we align our efforts with them closely. We understand what problems must be addressed immediately and what can be addressed later.

The employee corrects quickly. We demonstrate an ability to recognize mistakes and react appropriately.

The employee knows himself or herself. We are aware of our own strengths, which we leverage to maximum impact, and our weaknesses, for which we devise ways to compensate by leaning on each other as a team.

Employees exercising good judgment are ones who think first and then align their actions with established organizational priorities. These individuals consistently make good choices for the students, parents, and colleagues whom they serve.

Culture Element 4: Employee Utilizing Great Communications

The employee is in tune. We value people who are great listeners and have great empathy for and understanding of others. We recognize effective communication is as much about knowing when and how to share input as it is about having valuable input to share.

The employee is articulate. We communicate clearly and concisely, and we understand that what we say is as important as how we say it. We understand we must use kindness and respect in all communications—written, phone, and face to face.

The employee is honest and direct. We are truthful, candid, and consistently acknowledging both what we are doing well and what we are not doing well. We speak with good purpose when addressing others, especially when we have offended others or when others have offended us, bringing closure with kindness and tact.

The employee is transparent and forthcoming. We value people who understand the need to be transparent and forthcoming. Our culture is not defined by policy and procedure but by an openness wherein individuals are vulnerable and willing to make a few mistakes, with the knowledge that they need to be willing to own the victory or failure. Team members will be public in their ownership.

The employee is courageous. We question actions that do not align with our values and voice concerns, even if they are controversial.

Team members' communication with others is central to overall success. Sometimes extra training is necessary for employees who have a lot of face-to-face interactions with students, parents, and colleagues.

Establishing a customer service team that is tasked with creating a customer service policy, procedures, and ongoing training for team members is a best practice. For instance, these employees consider topics such as the importance of identifying the proper use of a telephone call versus electronic communications, as they can lead to an unfortunate disconnect or misunderstanding.

CULTURE IN ACTION

With passion, impact, judgment, and communication as the foundation of the workplace culture, the organization and its employees have the building blocks in place to now target staff development opportunities that align with these elements.

These culture points build and reinforce the skills the organization values and encourages in the workplace for all individuals. Employees, in turn, connect with students whose goals are to think critically, communicate effectively, and achieve academically across all grade levels.

The school culture is a critical element in promoting academic success for students and the community who are served by the public charter school.

A leader's ability to successfully communicate the values of the established culture can be most effective when each element is targeted, discussed, and promoted individually. A leader might choose to focus on one culture element annually while creating opportunities for dialogue and discussions around the topic to enhance the team's understanding of and investment in that specific culture point.

As an example, when it comes to judgment, a leader can define the term and the elements around that topic in a team meeting. This can start as a discussion at one meeting, and then at a follow-up gathering, a leader can introduce a book or resource specific to the element of judgment.

Having team members continually discussing an element of your culture over the course of an academic school year drives home the point that what you value as an organization is worth the time and investment in resources.

Leaders who are willing to spend time on training and conversation about the organization's culture increase the likelihood that all employees will understand and embrace those culture elements. Employees with a personal connection to the culture are likely to have higher job satisfaction knowing that they play a direct role in the school's success.

When defining your school culture, you can begin with a list of values or elements that you believe in or have seen successfully implemented in other organizations. As a leader of your charter school, you can then implement a workplace culture by explaining, showcasing, and detailing the value of each element to your team for their understanding and endorsement.

Leaders should also pull together a group of parents, teachers, and community members to help define the culture points for the organization. These strategic and focused gatherings help draw the collective enthusiasm of individuals in defining the workplace culture. These people will participate in the process from the ground up in what will become the sustaining force for the learning community.

These efforts create opportunities to build trust, share ideas, and strengthen the relationship between the leader, the employees, and the school community.

Having an open and honest dialogue concerning values and cultural elements starts with a leader being open to employee feedback. A leader who is unable or unwilling to take and process feedback is in a place where he or she has stopped growing professionally. All employees, including the leader, need and should value feedback on their ideas, their demeanor, and their impact within the workplace.

In addition to this essential groundwork, creating, sustaining, and valuing a workplace culture also provides all employees with incentives, expectations, and direction on what is acceptable when it comes to their performance.

Employees like to know what is expected and how they individually can impact the goals of the organization. The culture elements provide a touch point that individuals are looking for in their daily interactions with students, parents, and colleagues.

In the absence of strategic thought and effort in developing this area of the school, a detachment will encroach into all areas of the organization. A lack of leadership results in a culture being established that may or may not embrace and promote academic success and the intended school mission.

In most cases, when apathy and arrogance dominate the school culture, fragmentation will occur. This does not promote academic success for students, nor does it create a cohesive and caring workforce within the organization. If anything, this kind of culture promotes a personal lack of accountability for the students and the employees within the learning community.

Leadership makes all the difference in imagining, establishing, and maintaining a productive and meaningful organizational culture that drives educational outcomes and employee productivity.

Leaders should be looking for ways to reinforce and infuse these elements into all areas of the organization and help drive the conversation from suggestion to action.

CULTURE AND THE EVALUATION PROCESS

As a charter school leader, you likely have control over many aspects of your program, including, but not limited to, the employee evaluation process. By utilizing culture elements like passion, impact, judgment, and communication, you can develop your employee evaluation process to produce a culture score for each value that can be tracked and evaluated annually.

Annual evaluations can be used with administration, teachers, and classified staff by peers, parents, or students, depending on the type of information sought. Questionnaires can also be extremely valuable for the coaching and mentoring of your workforce.

All team members, from the executive director to the credentialed and non-credentialed employees, should be encouraged to grow in their positions.

Here are some examples of how the four culture elements of passion, impact, judgment, and communication are implemented using a rubric scoring system at The Classical Academies (see table 1.1):

Table 1.1.

Element 1: Passion

Expectations : *Cares deeply, tenacious, inspiring, selfless, brings heart.*

Score :	*1 Far Below Expectation*	*2 Below Expectation*
	3 Meets Expectation	*4 Exceeds Expectation*

Element 2: Impact

Expectations : *Accomplishes incredible things, follows through, is results-oriented, is biased toward action, increases impact of others.*

Score :	*1 Far Below Expectation*	*2 Below Expectation*
	3 Meets Expectation	*4 Exceeds Expectation*

Element 3: Judgment

Expectations : *Does "right things," is intentional about work, prioritizes well, corrects quickly, knows self.*

Score :	*1 Far Below Expectation*	*2 Below Expectation*
	3 Meets Expectation	*4 Exceeds Expectation*

Element 4: Communications

Expectations : *Communicates clearly and concisely, is truthful, speaks with good purpose, is a great listener.*

Score :	*1 Far Below Expectation*	*2 Below Expectation*
	3 Meets Expectation	*4 Exceeds Expectation*

When the culture elements are part of the employee's annual evaluation, a leader has increased the level of importance placed on sustaining that culture by holding employees accountable for their actions.

This simple and effective use of the elements of your school's culture will give your employees feedback about their level of participation in sustaining the organizational culture. Every employee needs to connect his or her actions to sustaining the workplace culture.

Another area to infuse the culture elements to encourage participation is with your employee incentives and awards. For example, when considering whom to recognize, at The Classical Academies we ask these questions:

1. Who on your team has exercised great *JUDGMENT*?
2. Who is the most *PASSIONATE* player on your team?
3. Which employees did a great job *COMMUNICATING* with a parent, leading to a great solution or meaningful outcome?

4. Which employees made a great *IMPACT* this school year with the best academic gains for their students?

These are simple and effective ways to honor your employees, restate the importance of culture, and highly value those who embrace and personalize the organizational culture. Plus, employees love and value being recognized in front of their peers. So at your monthly team meeting, highlight the culture element and present a certificate or two for those employees who have exhibited the behavior you are looking for in your workforce.

Rewards and recognition are a simple way for leaders to highlight the importance they personally place on the culture and its impact on the students, parents, and learning community.

As the leader establishing a school culture, be certain that you are championing the cause and living the elements you want to see in others, too.

Utilizing the culture elements mentioned previously as an example, ask yourself a few questions.

Are you a passionate leader?

Do you communicate well?

Do you exercise good judgment in what you say, disseminate, or post online?

Are you making a positive impact on students, parents, and the school community?

How are you being evaluated — and are your culture points in your annual review, as well?

These are simple ways for a leader to set in motion the steps needed to create and establish a successful workplace culture. With the goal in mind of benefiting students, parents, and all employees, spend time considering your culture or the one that you would like to create for your school or learning community.

Be sure to develop a positive culture that will drive individual academic outcomes for students as well as increase employee job satisfaction and productivity for all charter school personnel.

LEADERSHIP POINTS TO REMEMBER
REGARDING SCHOOL CULTURE:

1. Establish a school culture that is definable, manageable, and means something to you personally.
2. Collaborate with students, parents, and fellow team members in selecting culture elements for your learning community. This process facilitates ownership and personal connection to that culture.

3. A culture will be developed with or without a leader's effort. Make sure that you invest the time and energy into creating and sustaining your school culture.
4. To achieve a successful learning environment, school culture must connect students, parents, and personnel to well-defined and measurable elements.
5. Your school culture is a topic of discussion that should be regularly incorporated into meetings, gatherings, and award presentation, and should be a part of your annual employee feedback and assessment.

TWO

Mission Magic

"Pursuing a mission without achieving results is dispiriting; achieving results without a mission is meaningless." —Frances Hesselbein, president and CEO of Leader to Leader Institute

In 1976 CBS television aired the live-action science fiction children's series *Ark II*. The show was part of the Saturday morning lineup, and 13-year-olds like myself ate up the cool gadgets, futuristic setting, and jet-propelled backpacks.

This children's show featured three scientists, a talking chimpanzee, and their adventures in the post-apocalyptic landscape of 25th-century Earth. The Ark II scientists vowed to rebuild what had been destroyed. "This is their achievement . . . Ark II, a mobile storehouse of scientific knowledge, manned by a highly trained crew of young people. Their mission: to bring the hope of a new future to mankind." A noble adventure tied to a stated and specific mission.

Prior to the 25th century, in 1991, the State of Minnesota created legislation that allowed the establishment of America's first public charter school with the hope of improving the vast landscape of public education by allowing independently operated public schools of choice.

This was the first time that a legislature had the vision to bring competition to the educational landscape in America for the betterment of everyone involved. In 1992, California followed suit and became the second state to open charter schools.

So what has been achieved since that "Charter Ark" launch in 1991? According to the National Alliance for Public Charter Schools (www.publiccharters.org) March 15, 2013:

- 6,400 charter schools are currently in operation nationwide
- 2.3 million students enrolled in these public schools of choice

- 42 states (including Washington, DC) have charter schools offering options to students and parents
- Mixed achievement successes from state to state

When you think about it, charter school leaders are like those "scientists" helping to build better options for students and parents. Charter school employees are involved in a movement that is changing the educational landscape of your community, region, and state.

Much like the mission of Ark II, charter schools are bringing hope for a new future in public education. This is only possible when a leader, working with his or her team, is able to specifically define and implement a mission for his or her school.

DEFINING THE MISSION

A mission statement should be short, specific, and inform everyone of what will be accomplished on a consistent and continuous basis. It has been said that "as long as you are meeting your customer's needs, no one is looking at your mission statement."

The cartoonist Scott Adams used his character Dilbert to share his perspective on a mission statement by saying, "A mission statement is a long awkward sentence that demonstrates management's inability to think clearly" (The Dilbert Principle 1996).

Funny? Awkward? True?

The time and effort that a school leader exerts in creating a mission statement reflects its importance, reflecting whether what it says matters and whether what it says will be supported and accomplished.

As a public charter school, both of these efforts are paramount to ongoing and sustainable success for students, colleagues, and the entire learning community.

If you are thinking about starting a new charter school in your community, it is key that you have a specific academic focus targeted at a specific population of students. With all public schools, no singular format will meet the academic needs of all students attending.

This is one reason that a group of parents, educators, or community members will seek to open a charter school: to meet the specific academic needs of a targeted population. This dictates the necessity of creating a specific mission statement.

During the new school planning process, a mission statement will be crafted. This will be included in the founding charter document to share with parents seeking school choice and to provide to the community in order to distinguish the school as a unique learning community within the context of other public schools.

A leader should be able to state the school's mission clearly to explain how this new school will differ from others and how it will meet the academic needs of students targeted to attend.

During the planning process for a new school, the words and phrases selected to create the mission statement should be specific and strategic. This group of words and phrases will clearly define who will be served, how they will be served at the charter school, and what should be expected as a result.

In a quick review of most public school district websites and individual public school websites, a mission statement can be found. Whether or not this statement influences decisions and spending priorities is anyone's guess. It is the intention of the leader at a charter school to utilize his or her mission statement as the foundation by which all decisions should be made.

Take any school's mission statement and break it down. Are there elements that focus on students, parents, or the school community?

What are the elements that tell a parent whose student will be enrolling what will be expected of them?

What will be accomplished?

And what results should be expected?

A charter school mission statement should include these elements and inform and answer these questions in a few simple statements or phrases.

Now, if you are a charter leader working in a school that has operated for several years and has an established mission statement, how are you using this information to manage the organization and how are decisions being made as a result?

Chances are, you are doing this without even thinking about it, but making a concerted effort will ensure that the founding principles of the school are supported and adhered to continuously for the benefit of the students whom you serve. A leader's action in this area continues the legacy by staying focused on the established mission, even decades after the start of the school.

As a charter leader, you may have been fortunate enough to be involved in the creation and founding of your charter school. You may have had the opportunity to write or work on the charter document for your school. If so, you were in the trenches when the passion, vision, and tenacity all aligned to define why the school was being created.

What niche were you attempting to fill?

What population or demographic of student were you looking to serve?

What innovative academic program were you seeking to establish?

These are all the elements that help define your school's mission.

Even if you were not there at the founding of the program, your role as the charter school leader is to know, embrace, and promote that school mission with students, parents, and colleagues. Your understanding of the mission will clearly impact the program.

If the school's mission is set aside, a leader runs the risk of having a nominal program when it comes to impact, growth, and connection to students and their learning.

REVISITING THE MISSION

As the school leader, it is incumbent to visit the mission statement from time to time with your team, too. They, like you, need to be immersed in a discussion of why you are in business, what you are there to accomplish, and why the mission is important.

Your team's understanding of the school's mission is a critical piece in your charter school success story. Having each and every team member strengthen their understanding of the school's mission directly improves their alignment and adherence to the founding principles of the organization.

The school's mission is also a factor as you look to grow the program and possibly bring in new elements to add to the program. Using the mission as a filter, how will this new program or element align to the mission statement for the school?

How will this new activity further that established mission?

What you will find is that not straying from your foundational principles will allow you to maintain that original focus placed on students, parents, and your unique school community.

What makes your charter school unique should continue to be grounded in and defined by your school's specific mission.

As the school enters the charter school renewal process—in California that is every five years—the school leader should revisit the mission statement and the impact it has or hasn't had on the learning community.

This is a great time to set up a community meeting where current employees, committed parents, your board of directors, and the school leader should discuss the mission statement and the alignment of the school's program to this document.

This discussion should include the possibility that the mission statement needs to be edited, changed, or redefined.

A leader's openness to making small or major changes to the mission statement is a telling moment in his or her leadership. Having a school leader who is unwilling to make changes is a sure bet that a charter school will lessen its impact when it comes to serving students and the community.

A leader needs to know his or her students and the effectiveness of school events and activities, and have a pulse on educational trends as they relate to the charter school. Gauging these elements, and the changing landscape of public education, dictates that making a course correction, detailed in an updated mission statement during the charter renewal process, can be time well spent.

During a community or team meeting, a school leader should be asking parents and team members about the effectiveness of the school's mission and its impact on individual students and the overall school community. In these comments a leader should find positive and key connection points that align both audiences. In the event that you discover that parents hold a different perception of the impact of the school's mission than that of your team, the alignment is off and needs correcting.

If you have teachers, or other school employees, out of alignment with the stated school mission, this will impact student learning and outcomes, too. If a school has a teacher or team member who lacks understanding, is out of sync, or works outside the established expectations created by the mission, there will be consequences.

Your team needs to know, embrace, and understand that their actions and attitudes need to align with the stated school mission.

Collectively your team should be striving to fulfill that established mission by working toward a common goal, ensuring that alignment is attained and expected school-wide student results are kept in tune with the stated mission.

Any revisions to a school's mission statement should come at a time when the school's founder or founders are available to help the current leader and workforce know the reason or reasons why a specific mission statement was chosen for the school.

It is optimal to have these individuals share their perspectives with the group to ensure that everyone is on the same page with the methodology and process that was in play at the time the statement was created and adopted.

If the original founder or founders are no longer associated with the school or are unable to take the time to review the stated mission's methodology and share a perspective as to why it was chosen, this should not stop a leader, working with concerned stakeholders, from formulating some changes to the school's mission.

As a charter school leader, you should be cognizant that when the school originally started it was serving a few types of students, and over time that school population may have changed. With these changes in student demographics, it may be time to change the mission statement altogether to remain relevant and aligned with whom the school is now serving.

A school leader should be asking himself or herself some fundamental questions when it comes to rethinking the school's mission:

1. Has the educational climate of the community changed over time?

2. Have the socioeconomic conditions of your school community changed over time?
3. Have the enrollment demographics of students, and their families, attracted to your program changed over time?
4. Have the academic outcomes for students increased over time?

A quick survey of your historical student data will be telling and help answer these questions. It is also possible by reviewing your annual parent satisfaction survey, or by including some specific questions in the next survey that will be distributed to parents to align with the charter school's renewal.

GETTING EVERYONE ON BOARD

Another factor to consider in schools where you have a working board (versus a policymaking board) is that governing members may have specific ideas that they would like included in the review process for the school's mission. Charter school boards do, and should, play an active role in the establishment or rethinking of a school's mission statement.

Since these individuals, working with a school leader, are ultimately responsible for the financial and academic health of the organization, it is incumbent upon this group to be active in the final draft of the mission statement. Their actions and decisions should also be in alignment with this document once completed.

Governing board members who are mission driven lead through their decisions and actions, and uphold the mission by prioritizing spending and management decisions that align and support the organization.

Much like employees who do not have a firm understanding and appreciation of the school's mission can move in a direction that ultimately results in compromises, a board member or members can do the same. The actions of a board and its members can change the course of the school completely. Having the mission as the cornerstone of how and why a charter school is in business allows the board to govern effectively.

The school leader is well served when he or she takes the time annually to include an update to the governing board with either a presentation on the school's mission, or elements of the school's mission and the impact on the program that he or she is experiencing. Having a team member, parent, or student share specifics of those accomplishments as part of the presentation keeps the focus on what is best for students and the individual impact the school is having.

This is also a great opportunity for a leader to elevate a student, parent, or fellow team member into a position of sharing information with the board of directors. A school leader's effort to include others in the updating process speaks to how he or she is mentoring or training others to take on responsibilities on the school site.

Sure, the school leader is responsible for the day-to-day management of the organization, and helping others succeed is a priority that can include having them speak on behalf of the leader to provide additional evidence of success being achieved.

What better way to keep a school community mission driven than to have students, parents, and school employees memorize the school's mission statement.

As school leaders visit classrooms, attend school events, and participate in activities, they can display leadership by reciting the mission statement as part of an address, awards ceremony, or school celebration.

Make it part of the start of the school day by reciting it after the Pledge of Allegiance as an entire school body. Having the mission statement incorporated into the day-to-day activities at the school site helps align the community and promotes academic excellence for students.

ESSENTIAL MISSION PROOF POINTS

As a charter school leader, here are some thoughts for you to consider.

Is the mission statement printed and on display in your school's office, classrooms, lunch area, or play area?

Is the school's mission prominently displayed on the school's website?

Is it printed on the school's official business stationery or business cards?

Is it listed in the employee or parent handbook?

If you are serious about your school's mission, then have it available in multiple locations and in multiple formats.

A few ways to get students and parents mission minded is to:

1. Sell binders or folders to students that include the school's mascot and mission statement.
2. Sell paperweights or magnets (assorted merchandise) to parents featuring the mascot and mission statement.
3. Sell spirit T-shirts to students and parents that include the mascot and mission statement.
4. Sell license plate holders with the school name and mission statement embossed on them for student and parent vehicles.
5. For a school with sports teams, sell merchandise embossed with the school's mascot and mission statement.

All of this adds up to keeping your mission statement accessible and memorable to the school's students, parents, and employees.

If a leader expects people to know the mission, be strategic in featuring it in places where they are likely to see it.

Another idea is to have every school employee include the mission statement after his or her signature that accompanies every e-mail. Now, the impact of that information is magnified as students, parents, vendors, and other organizations get numerous e-mails from your team and see that mission statement repeatedly throughout the school year.

Have a contest from time to time to encourage your community to be mission minded. Stop a student in the hallway between classes and ask him or her to recite the school's mission statement to you.

At an all-team meeting, can one or more of your team members recite the mission statement, or are they just reading it off the wall plaque you installed last week? At a parent gathering or field trip, can one or more of these parents recite this key phrase back to you?

Consider the value in creating a mission-minded award or certificate that can be given out when students and employees exhibit actions that align with the school's mission. This intentional act by the leader to acknowledge "mission-like" behavior is time well spent and reminds the entire team of the value you place on the mission and the impact it plays on the day-to-day activities at the school.

A school community, committed to being mission minded, understands that its actions are aligned to promote individual academic success for all students. This community also has the ability to hold school leaders and governing boards accountable to operate schools and programs that focus on the individual needs of students.

This model of operation takes hold in newly formed charter schools where founding parents and committed community members have a vested stake in the survival of the school during its start-up and implementation phase. These parents, whose students are enrolled in newly formed charter schools, take steps to stay actively and meaningfully involved to ensure the school's success. They volunteer, donate, and spend time supporting the program on and off campus.

The school's success is based on their investment of time, skills, and professional abilities. These founding and first-year parents often take on a role to fulfill the school's mission, while leaders are busy managing the day-to-day operations or moving from fire to fire or incident to incident. The founding school leaders appreciate and embrace the extra support parents provide in most cases.

A leader serving at a school site where the parents firmly understand the mission can ensure that parents will stay focused on the work at hand. Interestingly, when the school moves into its second or third renewal, a larger amount of parents and students will begin to ask and press for changes to the program that may at times fall outside the school's stated mission.

It is during these times that a school leader must know and understand what is being asked and the impact on the overall program if he or she agrees to that student or parent request. Can or will that one decision impact the program? The easy answer is yes.

It is important for a leader to be reminded that your school is not for every student, nor can you change your school to meet the needs of every student. The mission is the foundation by which those decisions are decided, and in that, some things will not, and cannot, be changed to appease individual parent and student requests.

The strength of your leadership will be tested in these situations as you balance meeting specialized requests against what is the purpose of your school's mission and what your academic program currently has to offer.

Finally, it is very important that a leader has a process in place to train all incoming employees on the history, culture, vision, and mission for the charter school. This orientation is established so that all new team members are immersed in the reasons why the school is in business, whom they will be serving, and the elements that make the school or program unique.

This is a leader's chance to help all new team members gain a solid understanding of the uniqueness of the specific charter school and its mission to achieve success for those students whom it is targeted to serve.

If a leader fails to pass on the legacy of how and why the school was started, he or she runs the risk of lessening the impact of each new employee in harnessing his or her passion. New workers value knowing the history of the organization and how their skills and abilities will be used and added to the fabric of the school's success. The workforce is better served when it has a personal connection to the school's foundation.

Just like adding a new addition to a building, it may change the appearance of the structure and modify the original architect's vision for the facility. Or that same addition can be made and a passerby never knows a change was made. It can be the same with new employees.

Those who know, value, and understand the mission align and fulfill their part in helping sustain it through their accomplishments. Those who do not know, value, or understand the mission will move in a different direction, thus changing the organization through their actions.

So as a school leader, you must acknowledge the importance and value of a mission statement. You are also the one who should have a foundational knowledge of why it was created so your program will have the chance to greatly impact future students and families attending the school.

As the school leader, are you living like those young scientists on Ark II, bringing hope to students and parents?

As a charter school professional, I would venture to say, yes! Keep it up! What was begun at your school continues to improve, and the impact of your organization will be recognized as a result.

I recently purchased the complete series of *Ark II* on DVD. All 15 episodes are contained on four discs with a few special features. Let's just say that the cool factor that this one-time 13-year-old remembered has been replaced with loads of cheesiness! Special effects have come a long way since 1976, but so has my ability to understand the magic of a well-designed and implemented mission.

LEADERSHIP POINTS TO REMEMBER
REGARDING A SCHOOL'S MISSION:

1. Your mission statement is important, meaningful, and should define why you are serving students at your charter school.
2. A leader should filter decisions through the mission statement to ensure that priorities are aligned with established expectations.
3. A leader should be able to recite and explain the mission statement of his or her school to students, parents, and school colleagues.
4. A mission statement should be reviewed with each charter school term or renewal to evaluate its relevance to the school's culture and community.
5. A leader has a responsibility to stay mission minded so that his or her school maintains its focus on staying true to its foundational principles.

THREE

Parent Power: Harnessing Their Passion to Impact Your Program

"Successful people are always looking for opportunities to help others. Unsuccessful people are always asking, 'What's in it for me?'" —Brian Tracy, motivational speak and author

A school leader's greatest advocate is a satisfied parent. This satisfaction comes when a parent's son or daughter is succeeding in school both academically and socially. Parents offer encouragement and praise for a school leader, and his or her team, when this is accomplished.

When their son or daughter is not succeeding, that same friendly and connected parent can turn the tables on a school leader and begin to make demands that may or may not be within the control of the school leader to fix or change.

These are the times when a school leader needs to have developed the trust and confidence of parents in the management of the school program.

Trust and confidence is built when a school leader communicates regularly, provides updates on school operations and programming, and takes the time to meet individually with parents.

These meetings can be a casual gathering or a specific set time. Having the school leader available in a community area of the facility allows parents the opportunity to casually connect when they are dropping off or picking up their students. A leader's accessibility builds trust and provides parents an open door to ask questions or provide feedback.

With larger schools, it may be best to establish a standing monthly or quarterly gathering when the school leader is available. This is a great time for you to have a few topics to discuss where the school is looking for feedback on programming, events, and activities. This is also an op-

21

portunity to have parents ask questions and provide feedback on the program. Just by providing a meeting location and time to listen, parents will feel empowered—and you'll earn trust and gain good feedback.

Openness to advice is another great way for a leader to gain trust. Parents and students value a transparent and progressive school leader who welcomes open meetings to receive commendations and recommendations that lead to maximizing the potential of all students and make the school a better place for learning.

Parents should be viewed as trustworthy partners in the educational relationship that connects their students to the school. Teachers, the support team, and the school leader have an obligation to define, create, and maintain a trustworthy rapport with their parent community.

A parent who doesn't have a level of trust with his or her student's school will most likely play an ineffective role that does not promote or encourage his or her child to succeed at this school. The importance of a healthy and happy parent community cannot be underscored enough.

This is why a school leader has an obligation to foster and promote open communication to ensure that parents understand and embrace their role and its importance to the school community.

Part of this communication is to offer parents a role in your school community. Parents can and will make a commitment to the school when they know that their skills and abilities will impact the program and they have a sense of connection and belonging.

Parents by their very nature want to be involved in the lives of their children. It is up to the school leader to embrace their involvement and create a school culture that is welcoming and open to facilitate parent involvement.

Educational studies, policymakers, and advocates sing the praises of parents and their connection to a student's success in school. The people who taught their son or daughter to walk, tie his or her shoes, and ride a bike are the same individuals who play the greatest role in impacting their student's efforts to stay engaged and active, to fulfill their personal academic potential in school.

Harnessing this parent potential at your school makes what's possible, possible.

It should come as no surprise, but having active and engaged parents within an educational community who share their passion, skills, and investment of time contributes to a thriving school campus that promotes students' academic success.

Successful school models include the key elements of student commitment, parent involvement, and a faculty focused on relevant and progressive content delivery. Think of a spinning plate suspended on the tip of a rod implanted into the floor. The plate represents the student, the flexible rod the teacher, and the foundation, the parent. When the plate is spinning successfully, the rod is moving, too. The foundation remains firm in its support. The faster the plate spins, the more flexible the rod becomes. If the flexibility and movement of the rod cease, the plate begins to slow down, wobble, and eventually fall.

The relationship between the student and teacher is essential to success. Their ability to work together is much like the plate that spins effortlessly sitting at the tip of a rod. When things are working well, the flexibility of the teacher allows the students to soar as their individual academic needs are addressed and met. The student-teacher relationship must be grounded in the connection to the parent or guardian.

A student knows that the parent is supporting the teacher, and the teacher knows that the parent is supporting the student. This foundational element of the parent mirrors the analogy of the spinning plate and rod. The foundation is in place to support both, and when successful, the student excels and the teacher is free to focus on making learning relevant, progressive, and fun.

PARENTS AS VOLUNTEERS

With the move to innovate and open school programs to embrace parents, school leaders are being required to create opportunities for parents to serve and have an active and meaningful role at the school site. Engaging parents in the work at hand can be a daunting task for a school leader. Most leaders have questions as they start this process at their school.

How do you ask parents to play an active and meaningful role in your school community?

How do you value and reward their investment in the success of students and the school as a whole?

What elements of the school's program should a school leader consider turning over to parents, and in turn, free up their paid team of the tasks at hand?

Needless to say, it is a balancing act that every school leader needs to achieve.

So, part of a school leader's annual collection of data has to include gathering specific information about the parents, their interests, and their connections to the larger community.

What skills do they have?

What would they like to contribute?

What role would they like to play?

This is all information that can be gathered from each parent annually. Collecting information is one thing. Utilizing it is another.

It is important that a school leader has access to a system, a database, and/or an Excel worksheet where all this data can be placed and easily searched to match a parent's skill set with a specific school project.

If you have a parent who is willing to help with a field trip, do not assign him or her to volunteer in the school office.

If you have parents who want to volunteer in the classroom, don't assign them to help cut out clothing patterns for the school's spring musical production.

Matching a parent's particular request to a specific school project builds value for parents and creates a sense of connection because their skills are being used and valued by the program and its leader.

A school leader and his or her team should work together to create an inventory of needed services annually to support the program. What identified services at the school site can or will be accomplished by skilled parents?

Here is a list of examples of where parents can serve in a school community to benefit not only the school program but also the students who are enrolled.

- Advocacy supporter
- After-school club or sports advisor
- Art program volunteer
- Baker for events or fundraisers
- Birthday club class advisor
- Book fair organizer
- Bulletin board organizer/decorator
- Business donation solicitor
- Campus cleanup helper
- Development/grant writer, fundraising
- Field trip helper/organizer
- Inventory helper
- Lunch and recess helper
- Library organizer
- Music program volunteer
- Promotion event organizer
- Photographer for school events
- Room parent
- School office support
- School photography support
- Science fair support
- Staff and teacher appreciation organizer
- Testing proctor
- Tutoring
- Writing thank-you notes

When parents serve in a role where they have no previous experience or their skill sets are not a match for an assigned role, the school runs the risk of not having those parents return to volunteer in the future.

As a school leader, you can avoid setting up volunteers for failure by not putting them in a place where they are likely to be frustrated or overwhelmed by the task at hand. Managing parent volunteer efforts can happen with ease when your database is managed effectively and parents are serving in roles they enjoy.

Having parents as volunteers is a great way to have them involved in the school community.

PARENTS AS LEADERS

Another way to garner support is to have parents participate as leaders in the program. With some charter schools, a number of parents serve in governance and leadership roles within the school, including the board of directors, administration, faculty, and staff. In addition to serving in official leadership roles, one of the most important aspects of parent leadership is the ongoing feedback provided on the quality of the educational program.

Two-way communication is developed through personal relationships between parents and staff as well as the collection of data from the annual parent survey, which is used to evaluate and modify the school's educational programs on a continuous basis. A school leader, working with board members and other leaders in the program, can create an effective team when the needs of students are kept at the forefront of decisions and spending priorities for the school.

Most charter schools are started by concerned and passionate parents wanting an alternative school of choice in their community to impact their son or daughter. That passion is translated into parents leading the charge to create and establish a school by working with a local school district or county office of education to approve the charter school document and petition.

Where some charter schools run into trouble early on is when their board of directors, usually made up of parents, wants to manage the day-to-day activities of the school from the boardroom. Despite good intentions, this micromanagement by the board is counterproductive and will end with students and families dissatisfied—and will put the success of the school at risk.

Not all parents understand employment law or know how to manage a business, prepare or read a financial statement, or create a marketing plan. This is why it is critical that the board allow the hired and assigned school leader to manage the day-to-day operations of the school.

If you have parent board members who want to maintain an active and meaningful role in the school community on a daily basis, they need to understand that their role on the board ends as soon as the meeting ends. Individual board members do not wield power or make decisions on their own.

Having a school leader who is fearful of or being manipulated by a rogue board member or two will lessen the impact that leader is making for students, or worse yet, it will force that leader to tender his or her resignation. These leaders know how ineffective they have become from the constant interference of individual board members running a personal agenda to change the school's program and operation.

This is not the precedence a school board wants to set, and it is clearly not a model that promotes academic excellence for all students. Having parents as leaders in a school community can be very effective when they maintain their professionalism and credibility as board members.

Early on in a charter school's formation, a board can start as a working board—one that collectively makes decisions prior to a school leader being hired. Once that leader is appointed, the board needs to quickly move into a policy and procedural role to maintain oversight on issues of finance, academic standing, and parent satisfaction with the program by helping craft policies and procedures that support and uphold these activities.

Having and maintaining a strong policymaking board can help support the school leader by ensuring that procedures are being followed and adhered to in the day-to-day operation and management of the school.

This means that you, as the school leader, have a responsibility to keep your board informed with regular updates on programs, activities, meetings, and events. Having a board that is not well informed can lead to a serious breakdown of communication and program oversight. A leader does not want to place himself or herself in a position where his or her board is caught off guard by being out of the loop on school information, projects, and priorities.

Exceptional school leaders actively seek parents who would like to serve in leadership roles on a consistent basis to oversee projects, events, and activities. Having these volunteer leaders working in these areas allows for parents to contribute and for projects and priorities to be accomplished.

This is also a great time for a school leader to create and facilitate a group of committed parent leaders, or ambassadors, who can represent the school at open house events, back to school nights, and other social situations.

These are great opportunities for a school leader to ask these ambassadors to speak with prospective families and share their experience and positive perceptions of the school. Having parent ambassadors spend time with new families is an excellent way to maximize the goodwill in your school community.

Committed and satisfied parents love to talk about their experience and can help promote a program better than a well-executed marketing plan.

PARENTS AS PROMOTERS

Another way parents can help promote the school program is to post positive reviews online on websites that collect parent comments on local schools. One of the most popular sites reviewed by parents is Great-Schools (www.greatschools.org). A school leader should visit sites like these from time to time to review the posted comments from parents about their school. It is also a great motivator for the school team when the leader shares positive posts with the entire organization. Hearing directly from happy parents is something that every school employee enjoys.

If you were to discover a nominal or negative comment about the school online, take note. Parents will sometimes post something that they would otherwise never mention to a school leader personally. Posted comments are public comments.

If you want to see more positive comments posted online, ask your parents annually to visit websites like GreatSchools and post their positive comments about a teacher, event, or school activity. Having a handful of parents post their encouraging perceptions of the school will put those negative, and sometimes untruthful comments, in perspective for others to see.

If the school leader sees one or two negative comments about his or her school that center on a common theme, he or she should take the time to investigate these anonymous submissions if possible. It is unlikely that parents would be commenting on a similar situation without reason, so a leader should take these comments seriously and work to get to the bottom of them.

Having parents publically share their dissatisfaction about a teacher, event, or activity online can be detrimental to a school's impact in the community, as perceptions can be formed that don't necessarily represent what is happening at the school site. Correcting this misinformation is a leader's job and should not be taken lightly.

Usually on these sites there is a place for the school leader to place a comment or information about the school program. This is a positive way to tell about the school, its culture, and the impact it is having with students. For instance, you should not shy away from sharing the successes and the gains being made by students academically. It's also a great way to feature places where parents can serve in your school community and the roles they play in the school's success.

Most of these sites are free to use, so you should be actively seeking opportunities to share about your school and the impact your team members are making for the students whom they serve.

Parents can also increase their support for the school by calling a local reporter to share a story idea about a unique or special program or event being offered at their child's school. This idea, of course, would be coordinated with the school leader in advance to ensure that they are in alignment with the idea and are welcoming when the call from the local reporter comes inquiring about the information a parent shared.

As local reporters come and ask about the school, the leader should have a list of three to five parents who can speak highly of and specifically about the topic in question. A leader should ensure that these parents are prepped to guarantee that they stay on topic and provide the reporter with the most relevant information to bolster the story to benefit the school.

Parents should not be encouraged to be disingenuous or share misinformation. If and when this happens, it always comes back to haunt the leader, the school, and the program. When speaking with a reporter, remember the old adage, "Honesty is always the best policy!"

When it comes to dealing with the press, it is sometimes helpful for parents to write letters to the editor or submit a community perspective editorial to the local paper detailing elements of success they are finding at a specific school. Some of the best times to do this are on or near the school's anniversary, during National Charter Schools Week in the month of May, or when your state or regional organizations host a gathering of charter schools for a conference.

Utilizing parent voices to call attention to your school's success can be some of the best free press a school can receive. Like getting a referral from a friend for a trusted mechanic or doctor, a positive review from one of your parents to a potential family is invaluable. As a school leader, hearing reports of satisfied families is encouraging and helps you to know you are on the right track.

Parents are more than happy to endorse a school or educational program where their son or daughter is having success. Having a school leader make an endorsement request from time to time to a select, well-spoken group of parents can be a powerful use of human capital to promote and market the school.

Utilizing parent quotes in a school's advertising is also a way to personalize the message to the community about the greatness of the program and allow parents to be part of the outreach efforts to help grow the school's enrollment.

PARENTS AS TEACHERS

There are a growing number of hybrid charter schools that combine class-room learning, online learning, and independent study options as part of the students' academic program. These schools require an increased amount of parent participation due to the fact that these programs cater to those students who desire more independence in how, when, and where they complete their assigned schoolwork.

In these programs, schools and parents are forming educational part-nerships. These hybrid schools really view parents as educators since they are working closely with their son or daughter to guide, coach, and provide assistance in the completion of their academic assignments pro-vided by a credentialed teacher.

With hybrid programs, there is an established element of parent train-ing that the school takes on in helping parents become the best educators for their students. These charter schools embrace a model of support to parents as the primary educator of their children, and the school is there to provide tools, resources, training, and academic oversight. Creden-tialed teachers assign academic work to be completed and act as the guide on the side, helping parents and students fulfill their roles.

This partnership with parents requires closer communication and al-lows a school to define the roles of what will be assigned to the students, how the parent and program will work together, and what expectations will be required when it comes to oversight and the completion of the student's assigned work.

This unique partnership with parents is one where those parents wanting an active and meaningful role in their student's academic pro-gram can be facilitated when the school embraces this format and model of education.

Having parents actively involved in the academic program allows for collaboration between credentialed team members and vested stakehold-ers in the program. Parents know their children best and have a keen sense of what their students need and how they best learn. Having this information in a partnership with a school can be a powerful contributor to a student's academic success. In addition, teachers are able to gain a better understanding of students by having parents actively engaged in the educational process.

In some schools this partnership allows students to participate in classrooms for part of the week under the supervision of a teacher and work online or independently at home the other part of the week under the supervision of a parent or guardian. This collaborative model is one where students, parents, and teachers support one another and play an active and meaningful role in keeping all parties accountable in fulfilling their assigned roles in the partnership.

This educational model also embraces the idea of having parents mentor and train other parents. More experienced parents share their tips for success in working with multiple-aged children, those identified as gifted, or those students needing some academic modifications.

Just like most professionals who seek ongoing professional development opportunities to improve in their roles, these parents are seeking input and guidance from those who have successfully navigated a hybrid school program. Strengthening the role a parent plays in supporting his or her student in these programs is time well spent.

Parent-to-parent training can include sharing elements of child development strategies, how to structure your student's day, and how to organize a space at home to maximize learning for your child.

Some additional topics parents might share that move beyond the traditional academic program include food choices and their impact on learning, limiting media consumption, and scheduling daily outside activities.

Parents whose students have found success in these hybrid charter school programs enjoy sharing their wisdom and experience with other families. It is incumbent on a school leader to schedule trainings on a consistent basis by asking seasoned parents to volunteer their time in sharing their expertise with new parents in the program.

To improve the impact of trainings for the audience, a school leader should consider offering programming broken into age bands: K–3, 4–6, 7–8, and 9–12. This will allow parents to pick and choose which training meets their specific needs for the age of the student or students in their care.

Offering monthly or quarterly breakout training sessions on campus allows parents to invest in becoming better educational partners for their students while benefiting other parents in the process, too.

As with all charter schools, not all schools can or will meet the needs of all students. Hybrid charter school programs do serve a unique population of students and work to fulfill their established missions by collaborating with parents. These schools also benefit from sharing with parents the challenges and successes, knowing that the partnership is directly tied to how well the school is performing.

Parents in these programs take personal responsibility for how well their son or daughter is performing, knowing that they played a personal role in helping facilitate elements of the academic program.

There is a trend in traditional educational circles to view parents who want to play an active and meaningful role in their son's or daughter's academic life as "helicopter" parents. Some school leaders act as if having a parent who wants to help at a school site or serve in a classroom is a bad thing.

To the contrary—having committed parents strengthens the school program. A community of parents, school employees, and administrators working together creates a cohesive and solid foundation where learning happens and students thrive.

PARENTS AS FUNDRAISERS

Another benefit of keeping a database of parent interests and skills is to ask that special handful of parents to help with the school's development efforts. Parents know and have connections with local retailers, organizations, and corporations that can benefit the school program and the students whom you serve. Asking for gifts and donations can be a daunting task to some, even the school leader at times. Leveraging a few key parents to make requests can make all the difference.

Parents usually have the same shopping habits and visit the same stores week after week and month after month. By doing this, they are probably known at these locations. Taking a bold step to speak to a store manager or business owner to make a personal request sometimes is what is needed to have that retailer offer a free product or service for use at the school's raffle or fundraising event.

Now, if your passionate group of parents asks several local stores and organizations collectively, you can see the value of the donations that will be coming in to the school as a result.

Parents should only target to make requests of businesses annually. Asking a vendor or business owner too often can lead to having that avenue closed, as the business owner may feel that his or her generosity is being taken advantage of by the school. Parents that are business owners should be approached first. They should have a firsthand knowledge of the impact the school is having on their student, so that makes the task of asking so much easier with this group of parents.

Another thing to ask parents with business connections is to find out which businesses will match a donation from their employees. Some organizations and corporations will match an employee's donation to a school or nonprofit—so that check for $250 is now worth $500. Parents who are employed at larger organizations or corporations may not be aware of this benefit offered to them and need a reminder from the school to check into this employee benefit. Just a simple reminder can make all the difference.

Having your key fundraising parents commit annually to calling every family in the program to ask for a small or large donation is another way to harness the power of parents to help the school. Parents calling parents takes the pressure off the school team to make these requests. Parent-to-parent fundraising has a way of involving most families, since it is hard to turn down another parent making the request on behalf of all students.

Not every parent can be successful with this task, and that is why it is critical that only parents volunteering for this duty be considered after indicating that they wanted to serve the school in this capacity. This specific role in supporting the school should be kept to a manageable size for the school leader.

With most tasks, when you have "too many cooks in the kitchen," there can be chaos. Since vendor relationships are very important for the school, you should ensure that only the most qualified parents are involved in these annual fundraising efforts.

PARENTS AS ADVOCATES

From time to time, charter schools are faced with changing political climates—locally, regionally, and statewide. When this happens, having parents advocate for their high-performing school can be just what is needed to ensure that the conversation stays on what is best for students.

All too often the conversation turns to adults' needs, with contracts, salaries, tenure, unions, and seniority. Having parents speak to local boards, county officers, and state leaders helps push past the politics and put a face with a family who is enrolled in a charter school.

School leaders should have a set of parents who have been identified as wanting to help with political advocacy.

These are the parents who like to attend city council meetings to speak to local leaders about the new facility request that is pending and needs city council approval for the school to move forward.

These are the parents who love to call state leaders to express their approval or dissatisfaction with pending legislation and the impact it will have on their charter school.

These are the parents who love to make telephone calls to a governor's offices to share their pleasure about having their student enrolled at a charter school.

As an exceptional leader, you should encourage advocacy efforts among your parents. Having an active parent group will allow your school to create a reputation locally, regionally, and statewide as a community who cares, gets involved with issues, and makes a difference for students. These efforts also keep the pressure on for creating, replicating, and sustaining high-quality schools for every community. Each parent voice matters, and having a school leader encourage those voices to collectively speak creates a choir for change.

Now let's be clear, a school leader cannot express an opinion or tell his or her parent groups how to vote or what to say. Public schools cannot commit money or staff time to political causes. This is an inappropriate use of taxpayer resources. What a school leader can do is encourage parents to become familiar with legislation and its impact on charter schools. Having well-informed parents is an asset to a school leader and the school community.

Politically speaking, parent apathy is dangerous. Parent engagement is powerful.

Parents will continue to be a driving force behind great schools and the national movement to reform all public schools to better meet the specific academic needs of students in their care. School leaders and their teams will continue to make changes to programs to align with the needs of families whom they serve.

Charter schools will also continue to grow in stature and reputation in local communities, thereby continuing to gather momentum to drive change within the traditional system of public education.

School communities who embrace the role that parents play, and their importance to school success, are more likely to make continuous and measurable improvements annually. This is possible based on the commitment that parents have to their student and the program that is meeting their academic needs. You should never undervalue the commitment of parents, or the ends they will go to to help their student succeed.

As you keep honing your leadership skills, never forget that when parents are involved in the educational community, your academic program will stand out based on the commitment parents have to helping fulfill the school's mission. When a school leader makes the investment to know, embrace, and involve parents in his or her school community, students excel, parents' satisfaction increases, and the program grows as a result.

It is hard to keep a great school a secret when parents share their joy, the state shares the academic results, and the community starts asking that more charter schools be created to harness parents' commitment to see that all students have the ability to attend an enriching, engaging, and relevant public charter school of choice.

School leaders are obligated to invite parents in, ask for their commitment, and then work together to maximize the academic potential for all students. Parent engagement not only works, but it's also extremely powerful — and students, schools, and our communities are the beneficiaries of their investment.

LEADERSHIP POINTS TO REMEMBER REGARDING PARENT POWER:

1. A leader needs to embrace the fact that charter school parents want to be active and meaningfully involved in your school community.
2. A leader needs to harness the power of parents by having them serve according to their talents and abilities.

3. Parents are the best advocates for a high-quality charter school. A leader should encourage parents to write about, post, and share their student's success in their community. Parents can also have a powerful voice when kept aware of proposed laws and current issues of public policy regarding education.
4. Involved parents take personal ownership for a school and its success. A leader should encourage parent participation in leadership, activities, and school events.
5. A school leader needs to be aware of perceptions that parents have about the school, programming, and personnel. Negative perceptions must be discussed and dealt with immediately. A negative perception, even if false, can be damaging.

FOUR

Communication Connections

"Communication is the real work of leadership." —Nitin Nohria, dean of Harvard Business School

What to say and when?
What should be shared?
What should be kept in confidence?

When to communicate and what to communicate is a huge challenge for any leader. Managing your message is key to a leader's success.

A school leader without continuous and strategic communication is like a rudderless ship adrift in a vast open sea. A school community needs effective communication to ensure that priorities and expectations are shared and that parents feel involved and included. Failure to provide that communication leaves everyone underserved and uninformed. Leaders need to communicate information clearly, in a manner that promotes trust and confidence in your leadership.

A leader needs to remember the rule of thirds and apply it to his or her communications. One-third of your employees like change. One-third need time to understand change. One-third dislike change at all costs. All employees like routine and, in that, employees also value short and specific information being shared.

A school leader needs to remember that e-mail is intended to share short, specific, and relevant information. Avoid writing a book when a sonnet is needed. Any lengthy communications should be reserved for a face-to-face or phone conversation so that body language and eye contact can add to the conversation.

E-mail, by its very nature, creates an emotional disconnect and leaves the reader wondering, or assigning motive and emotional intent, to the sender regarding the message. A leader can avoid these situations by reserving specific times during the week to share information with one

35

person or several team members. These individual or group meetings can be a powerful and honest time for a leader to connect and communicate on matters of importance to all.

One of the biggest challenges a leader faces is mastering effective communication. With all the avenues available, what should be used and when? Most electronic communication may lend itself to convenience, but it may not necessarily lend itself to providing a leader an effective avenue for connecting with and inspiring a team. This is also the case when communicating with your parent community.

COMMUNICATING WITH YOUR TEAM

Think about the numerous e-mails a leader receives daily. The amount of e-mailed information from vendors, parents, students, team members, and community leaders is huge. There are requests, questions, general information, events, activities, and invitations. The barrage of e-mails can bury even the most organized leader.

This same leader needs to be cognizant of the number of e-mails he or she is generating and sending. Just because you can send it doesn't necessarily mean you should.

A leader should limit the amount of daily e-mails he or she is sending. Less is better, and in that, each e-mail should be strategic and meaningful when sent. A leader should be asking himself or herself three questions in preparing to send an e-mail.

1. Is it useful? Does my team need this information now?
2. Is it relevant? Do my team members need this information now as part of what they are trying to accomplish?
3. Is it important? Does this information need to be shared with the group in this manner versus a face-to-face meeting?

A leader should create a schedule that is communicated to the team on when they should expect written updates. These updates should be consistent and broken into manageable categories to help employees find and process these updates. Consider breaking your messages into three categories.

1. What you need to know this week.
2. Follow-up on past projects or priorities.
3. Future planning and projects.

This format and schedule speaks to a leader's strategic planning for written communications, with the goal of having an effective impact with his or her team. Your meeting notes should come quickly after the gathering to maintain the momentum of what was discussed and decisions that were made by and for the team.

Sure, information will come up during the course of the week that will need to be shared in a timely manner, but these e-mails should be the exception and not the rule. It is up to leaders to determine if they themselves should share or whether they should hand off to another team member to share.

Also, leaders should be mindful that they should let others communicate with the team on topics that fall under that specific employee's role and responsibility. Build trust on your team by sharing. In some cases, provide feedback but be willing to stand back and let individual members of your team shine.

In addition, as a charter school leader you ought to consider choosing one day of the week when you will share a team update.

Will it be Monday as you start the week to share a look forward and comment on the past week's success?

Will it be Friday to share the week in review, including relevant information for employees to prepare for a new week?

Will it be a Wednesday update to share what was accomplished the first two days and then include a look ahead?

Whatever day is selected, a leader should stick with it and be consistent with messaging so the team knows what to expect and when. Sporadic e-mails get lost and employees will miss key updates.

Remember that each employee is busy and your e-mails should be scheduled events on their calendars. As with most professionals, what is scheduled is a priority and gets done. What is not can get overlooked or forgotten. Keep your communications on their priority list. This comes with a leader being consistent.

Sending e-mails at all hours of the day and evening tends to speak to a leader's inability to focus and implement an effective communication strategy for his or her team. Most e-mail programs have the ability to store and send messages at a later time. This feature will allow you to compose an e-mail while the thought or information is fresh in your mind. These thoughts can arrive at 7:00 p.m. on a weekend or at 2:00 a.m. on a holiday. Both times are not good times to send that message to your team. The scheduling feature in your e-mail will help you capture the information now and launch that update at a later date or time.

Plus, another benefit to the launch later feature is that what sounded like a great idea at 2:00 a.m. on a holiday can later be edited or deleted before being disseminated to the team. Effective communication involves separating the good ideas from the great ideas. Make the most of your written communications by centering them on great information rather than just good information.

Remember that on every team you will have an overachiever or two who will monitor his or her e-mail accounts consistently. Evenings, weekends, and holidays are now open game with smartphones, message chimes, and vibrating units, so these employees will be reminded that you are working while the rest of your team is not.

For some, just getting that e-mail means that they should be reading it and responding immediately—even if they are on a holiday, weekend, or vacation. Having employees receive e-mails at all times of the day and night only showcases the fact that a leader does not have boundaries and spends too much time focused on work.

This communication practice also communicates to the team that your leadership requires a 24/7 focus. This may or may not necessarily be true; however, your actions impact the team and speak volumes about when and where you work.

You are leaving a digital trail that some talented employees on your team may or may not want to follow into leadership. Your behavior at 2:00 a.m. may be communicating that leadership comes at a price too high, which some may not want to pay. What talented team member have you scared off or turned off due to your communication patterns? A great reminder to you: everything speaks.

If your e-mail program doesn't allow for a send later feature, utilize the draft e-mail feature. Messages can be created, saved, and stored for later distribution. Another benefit of utilizing the schedule later or draft feature of e-mail is to allow a leader to reread communications before sending. What sounded good at 2:00 a.m. or over a three-day weekend may not now in the light of day with a clear head.

A great communication reminder for leaders is to utilize the subject line of the e-mail to set expectations so that employees know what to do with the information. If you want a response, ask for one in the subject line. If it is for information only, state that in the subject line, too.

Some employees, if not told what to do, will carry a burden to respond to each and every e-mail they are sent from a leader. This increases their workload and fills your inbox with unnecessary replies and responses. Your team doesn't need more work, and you don't need more to read.

SCHEDULING YOUR TIME

Effective communication comes with effective scheduling. A leader can be easily drawn into the perceived need to monitor his or her e-mail account with every notification. The e-mail arrives, it's read, and a reply is sent. Now if a leader just sits at his or her desk and watches the e-mail traffic, minutes turn into hours, and hours turn into days. What impact was missed while you sat their reading and answering e-mails?

A leader should schedule a focused and specific time daily to review and answer e-mails. Your team and your community should be told about these times. It sets expectations and makes the most of your time.

You can also process the value of logging out of e-mail to avoid the trappings of looking up every time a notification sounds with the arrival of a new message. Constantly monitoring e-mail is distracting and is a creativity killer for a leader.

If you carry a smartphone that allows access to e-mail, consider turning off that feature. The constant notification of a new e-mail arriving diverts your attention from parent and student meetings, school events and activities, and investing your leadership creativity into problem solving and program development.

If your e-mail application can be moved on your smartphone, consider moving it off the home screen so you are not distracted by it during your workday. In the event of something happening that needs your immediate attention, your team should know to call you with that information and not e-mail you. E-mail should be a priority, but not one that requires your attention during every moment of the workday.

With parents, students, and your community relying on e-mail to communicate with you and the organization, your communication plan should include a focused time daily to review and respond to e-mails.

Once every two hours, review your account quickly for any parent or student e-mails that may need immediate attention. Missing a priority e-mail now will create issues for a leader later.

A leader's proficiency in locating and responding to those essential e-mails is crucial to his or her effective leadership at the school site.

COMMUNICATING WITH PARENTS

It is an exceptional practice to always reply to parents in person or on the telephone in the event they have shared an angry or frustrated e-mail with you. Hearing a leader's words, showing empathy, and connecting emotionally with a parent after he or she has sent an angry or frustrated e-mail detailing a situation or incident is time well spent to bring a resolution to the situation.

One of the biggest mistakes a leader can make is not calling the parent immediately. Parents respond better when a leader calls or agrees to meet with them to hear firsthand their complaint or issue. Holding that e-mail and not responding in a timely manner only allows the parent's frustration and anger to grow. Putting off a call to listen and apologize doesn't serve you or the parent well.

Leaders run the risk of being criticized by the parent when they do not respond immediately. It is human nature to not always think the best of someone, and in that, an angry or frustrated parent is quick to tell others about the situation and their perception of your lack of care or concern. Failing to respond in a timely manner creates a bigger challenge for a leader in clearing up the perception that has been created as a result.

It's true that, as a school leader, you should be ready to apologize. Remember, students are in your care, but they are not your children. Parents have varying degrees of ownership when it comes to their student's academic success and their behavior. When either of those is in question, a leader needs to think about the fact that an impartial approach is needed while considering the parent's concerns.

Leaders should prioritize meeting with a parent or guardian and avoid writing back to answer a frustrated or angry correspondence. There is less risk of being misunderstood or misinterpreted in direct contact. Written communication lacks the feeling, emotion, and needed eye contact that can quickly bring closure to an emotional situation.

Leaders should establish the communication expectations for parents so that next time they will call or stop by when they have an issue or a question to discuss. Encouraging connection through communication is extremely valuable to successful leadership.

Sometimes when leaders think they are making progress, replying to an e-mail with that "message of best intentions" is misread and ends up making the situation worse. Parents and students need to know that you are an open and accessible leader. Hiding behind e-mails, or thinking that a quick written response to an angry or frustrated e-mail will bring closure to the matter, only helps widen the gap of miscommunication. This would be a poor choice for resolution and an ill-fated attempt at communication.

When dealing with all-important issues, e-mail should be your second or third communication tool behind utilizing the telephone or meeting face to face. Your ability to communicate as a leader should be enhanced by this practice, rather than compromised by a choice to utilize electronic communication that lacks a personal connection. The emotional investment you make into communicating effectively has a large payoff when you place a priority on verbal communication first.

COMMUNICATING ONLINE

Your leadership communication plan should include an online component as more and more families are utilizing social media to connect, share, and discuss their lives, their school, and their community.

Avoiding going online to connect with parents isn't always the best choice. The world of communication is changing, and your leadership should be changing along with it. Are you adapting to what parents need and how they communicate those needs?

For a school leader, being online at some point during the day, week, or weekend can be time well spent. It is there that you will often read praise, commendations, and recommendations coming from students, parents, and your employees. In addition, having a school policy on social media is a tool that helps set expectations for all employees, including the school leader, when posting and interacting online.

People are very willing to post information online that they may or may not be willing to share with you in a face-to-face meeting or gathering. Your job as a leader is to process the comments and either plan to privately respond, or keep the information for a time and place that is appropriate to respond. It goes without saying that in times of seeing bully behavior, comments derogatory to your team or school should be addressed immediately.

There may be a situation when students are voicing an opinion about one of your teachers. They may be discussing their lack of trust or lack of understanding with direction given on an assignment, or expressing sheer joy that they have this individual as their teacher. Each of these situations should and can dictate a separate response.

If you see a parent praising the school or a team member, share it. If you see a student praising the school or an individual, share it. A leader's job is to encourage and promote excellence on the team. Having access to parents and students through social media allows everyone to view open and honest comments. When something is praiseworthy it should be shared.

Leaders should be cautious with their online activity as students, parents, and the larger community are watching. Posted information doesn't ever go away, even if it is deleted. School leaders need to be reminded that they are public figures in their community. What they say, post, and respond to online can be seen—and it matters.

The digital footprint of a leader says a lot about what he or she values and who he or she is as a person. With the knowledge that school leaders are public figures, it is important to uphold personal integrity and honesty when interacting online. Using your position to encourage and promote excellence should also have you mentoring students and parents by setting an example of what you post personally.

A good communication model for leaders to follow with their online activity is the T.H.I.N.K. method.

T - Is it true?
H - Is it helpful?
I - Is it inspiring?
N - Is it necessary?
K - Is it kind?

As a leader processes his or her online postings and comments through this lens, it is likely that he or she will avoid embarrassment and misunderstanding later when parents, students, or complete strangers review his or her online activity. What you post directly reflects on your school, your employees, and your organization. If you don't like that reality, avoid social media.

This is also a great time to remind you that your community likes to know a little bit more about you as their leader.

What are your hobbies?
Are you married?
Do you have children?
Where did you go to school?
Where did you go on vacation?

Setting up a social media profile where students and parents can join you allows them to get to know you a little better and allows you to determine what information you want them to know about you personally.

The new normal seems to be that parents want to know their school leaders on more than just a professional level. Parents choose to entrust their children to your care and want to know who you are. They desire a personal connection to the school leadership to build trust through personal reference points; social media helps create this opportunity. Sometimes, shared activities such as a school team, a school play, church, community service, or other local activities can provide great opportunities for families to get to know a school leader and his or her family. There needs to be reasonable and healthy boundaries in this, however, as many school leaders wear many hats within a community—as parents, relatives, friends, and neighbors.

Each leader can figure out that personal and professional balance of what to share when online, but knows that trust and transparency are built when the leader is willing to show a personal side when dealing with parents in a professional setting.

School employees and volunteers on your team should know that the social media policy includes, "see something, say something." Since it is unlikely that you will be friends online with any or all of your parents and students, it is important for those who are their friend to say something when a derogatory comment is posted about an employee or the school.

Back to the point that parents and students post items that they may or may not be willing to say to a teacher or leader in a face-to-face meeting. In the event that a complaint about the school or personnel is posted, your team should be willing to inform you of the situation. Avoiding the post, and the subsequent postings by others, will not correct the misinformation or restore trust between the individual and the school community. A leader should use this as the catalyst to schedule a meeting to discuss the situation in an open and honest dialogue with the parent and students in question.

MEETING WITH YOUR TEAM

A leader should regularly meet with his or her team to share information and to maximize communication in a face-to-face setting. A leader should not be isolated or insulated from his or her team members. During these gatherings, the leader should balance talking and listening. There should be meetings when the leader is doing more listening than speaking. This is a great way to introduce a topic or situation and then seek the team's input.

The days of one leader or individual having all the answers, and being the keeper of all collective wisdom, is a management model of the past. Collaboration is an element that allows several individuals to play a part in a leader's success.

Meetings where individuals are invited to participate align with a leader's communication plan. An effective leader communicates the value of who is on the team and what they offer to improve the organization. Your ability to seek valuable input begins by developing a format where trust, truth, and boldness are welcomed. Once your team members know that they are trusted, they are more likely to offer bold ideas, recommendations, and commendations.

How do you build that trust? Let you actions match your words. When a team member offers a controversial or unconventional approach to dealing with a parent or student issue, acknowledge the contribution, make a note of it, and thank him or her for the feedback.

What you see as unconventional, others in the room will view as an open door to share their thoughts. Employees who witness their leader listening and considering an unpopular idea feel empowered to open up and share their thoughts, too.

A leader's ability to effectively communicate should be balanced between using face-to-face, public, and electronic formats to share information. In the age of information, leaders need to understand how and when their parents and students like to communicate and in what format. Knowing what connects with your community is essential to the effectiveness of your messaging.

Sharing an annual update at a public meeting might be one idea. Sharing that same information in a video posted on the school's website might be another. Expensive video and sound equipment are not required in this day and age. Most laptops and smartphones have all the necessary features to create a high-quality finished product that your community will appreciate.

One of the benefits of a posted video is that parents can later return to view it again or multiple times. If they missed your community meeting, or need to be reminded of certain facts, having this resource available allows them access to what you said, and how you said it. The video format also adds that emotional element that is often missing in written communications.

School leaders can take a few minutes from time to time and shoot a candid video that expresses their thoughts on student achievement, budget and fiscal issues, or school growth, programming, and accountability. Video is an inexpensive way to communicate quickly and effectively.

Video can also be used to impact your team in a special and meaningful way. A leader can easily utilize this format to cover or highlight information for the team outside the established face-to-face gathering.

This is also a great time for you to remind your employees of some behind-the-scenes projects or items you may be working on. Employees like knowing some of what is happening in your world so that they feel part of the bigger picture.

Utilizing this format is also another way to build trust on your team. Be willing to share some confidential information with them, too. Allow them to keep your confidence. As President Ronald Reagan once stated, "Trust but verify!" (December 8, 1987 remarks on signing the Intermediate-Range Nuclear Forces Treaty).

As stated earlier, a leader should not be scattered or sporadic with his or her communication. If you choose to utilize video, pick a day and time when your employees can expect to hear from you on a consistent basis. This strategic approach will allow your team to focus on your information and to know the priority you place on communicating with them. Once you have this schedule in place, employees will come to expect a message from you.

One idea is to pick a Friday to end the week with a video message and lay the groundwork for the following week's schedule of events and activities. This allows your team to prepare for the coming week, and you have set the tone for what they can expect.

Another idea is to send your video message every Monday to cover the past week's accomplishments and to set the tone for the coming week. The overall impact of your video message will increase as employees come to expect and look forward to your messages. But remember, when you pick a day, stick to it.

Leaders need to review the use of video much like they would in sending a memo to the team. Memos are usually topic specific and to the point. Videos should follow the same format.

Be sure to have your topics laid out in advance or you might begin to ramble. At that point, your video will move from topical, to trivial, to boring. Once the videos move to rambling and boring, you have lost the value in communicating in this format. Your team will tune out, and your messages will waste their time and yours.

Another creative idea is for the leader to be in different places each time he or she creates the video. Utilizing the "Where's Waldo?" approach can be a great way to add interest to your weekly update and keep employees guessing as to where it was filmed. A classroom, the parking lot, and outside the front office are all great locations and show a leader's creativity in updating his or her team weekly. As I often travel for work, I like to show where I am, and what I am seeing and doing. When our students take class trips to Sacramento and Washington, D.C., I have been known to include them in the weekly posts. Be creative, concise, and relevant. An important aspect of effective communication is the ability to have fun, and remember that video picks up your joy or your discomfort with the process.

ESSENTIAL COMMUNICATION PROOF POINTS

Your value as a leader is directly tied to your ability to communicate. Take the time to ask yourself a few simple questions as you establish these essential communication proof points.

How are you connecting with your community?
How do parents feel about you and the program?
How do parents feel about the school's events and activities?
Are you gathering feedback annually?
Have you created an annual survey to gather meaningful data for you and your team?

An annual survey should include questions in five key areas to give you and your team meaningful feedback:

1. Curriculum and instructional program.
2. Parent/school communications.
3. Special events and programs.
4. Customer service.
5. Overall satisfaction with the school and its educational program.

As part of your annual parent satisfaction survey, include a section on parent communications. Ask a few key questions to help set your communications plan annually to align with their needs. For example, include questions like:

1. How do you best like to receive information on school activities? Handouts? Website? School Facebook page? Other?
2. Would monthly messages from the school leader be of value to you? What topics would you like covered?
3. Do you use social media? Facebook, Twitter, LinkedIn, other?
4. Do you have a smartphone or laptop?
5. Do you have an e-mail address that is checked regularly?

Along with surveys, a leader should consider a standing open meeting with families twice a year. These meetings move the leader from behind the desk to an open and accessible gathering. These meetings also move a leader to work on the transparency of his or her organization. If you are seen regularly in public, trust is built—and your approachability is increased.

Plan a community meeting in the fall and a second gathering in the spring. This format will allow new families to get to know you at that first meeting. Plan topics to be shared at that meeting focused on this group and publicize it in that manner.

Your second meeting should be billed as a school update open to all families. Your spring meeting will provide longtime families in the program a chance to ask follow-up questions regarding your past all-school communications and updates on any programming changes or highlights.

Use these open meetings to listen more than you speak. Those parents that have braved the weather, missed dinner with their children, or gotten off work early to attend your meeting value their personal investment in education—and you should, too. Make the most of their time by listening to their commendations, recommendations, and feedback.

It is in meetings like these that trust is built when participants know that you are open and honest and value their feedback. Have a fellow team member attend the meeting to take notes. This will allow you to collect items to follow up on after the meeting.

As the leader, if you are busy trying to personally take notes, you will undoubtedly miss something. Leave that administrative duty to others so that you are present and engaged with your audience.

Unscripted open gatherings with a group of parents can be unnerving, but your willingness to provide the venue and opportunity speaks volumes to the transparency you desire to create for the students, parents, and those in your extended educational community.

Parents want time with their leaders, and these scheduled gatherings open up communications that may never happen in a one-on-one meeting. People will sometimes say something in a public setting, feeling an alliance with others, and their boldness can provide valuable feedback that is needed.

An effective community meeting should include a brief introduction, a welcome to those in attendance, and then a general overview of what you want to accomplish with the time. Meetings minus assigned objectives and outcomes tend to ramble and exceed their scheduled time. Make the most of your face-to-face time with community meetings. This is your chance to be specific with your communication for the benefit of you and your parents.

A good rule of thumb for public meetings is for a leader to spend half of the time asking the audience a few probing questions about the program. As you prepared your topics prior to the event, be mindful that parents will have questions. How will you address some of those possible questions in your presentation? This gathering may also be a great time to survey the parents on possible upcoming enhancements or changes to the program.

The second half of the meeting should be set aside for individual questions. Begin that second half by thanking your audience for listening, then open the time for questions on what you have covered. Remember, some in the crowd have questions on items not covered. It is statistically proven that what one person is thinking is shared by many. The question-and-answer period of your program will prove one of two things:

1. You understand your community and know their thoughts and feelings on your program and organization.
2. You do not know your community and are surprised by the questions and feedback about the program and organization.

If you are a longtime site leader and find yourself surprised by the recommendations and information shared, you are either an isolated leader or not in tune with those in your community. Your effectiveness and impact will be compromised by not being in alignment with the community you are there to serve. Remember the important words of business leader Ken Blanchard, "Feedback is the breakfast of champions" (August 17, 2009 HowWeLead.org).

As with most questions, they lead to others—and what started as positive statements about the school culture can quickly turn to a specific school employee's behavior. These are times when a leader needs to know what to say and when to say it. Never be afraid to defer or let the individual and audience know that you can or cannot answer a specific public question. Most should be aware of the fact that personnel issues are not for public comment or discussion. Also as a leader, there is nothing wrong with not knowing a specific answer to a question. A powerful statement that can serve you well is, "I don't know, but let me check on that for you."

SOME FINAL THOUGHTS ON COMMUNICATION

A leader's willingness to admit that he or she doesn't know something is not a sign of weakness but rather strength. Making something up on the spot doesn't serve the leader or the community. Leaders should be willing to admit what they do not know and not compromise their effective communication or messaging with parents, students, or the community.

After each public meeting, a communication should be sent to the overall school community to detail what was covered, any action items, and what recommendations or commendations were shared.

These messages are part of an ongoing campaign to keep your parents and community engaged in the organization's mission, vision, and annual goals.

Remember, each communication to parents should be relevant, meaningful, and important. Don't send messages that fall outside these parameters.

When it comes to communicating in a school setting, a leader needs to gauge what to send — and when to send it. Too many e-mails weekly tend to be lost as parents begin to tune out multiple messages with overlapping information on school events, report cards, lunch updates, programming changes, conferences, and back to school night announcements.

As discussed earlier, effective leaders will process the impact of calling parents versus sending a mass e-mail. Electronic communication may lend itself to disseminating information more quickly, but to maximize the impact with parents, a telephone call should be made from time to time by a teacher or school employee to parents. The human element of communication can never be replaced.

It is also great for school employees to hear that surprised and thankful voice at the end of the line. We have all become desensitized by the electronic world in which we live, so having a caring voice talking about an individual student is refreshing to a parent or guardian.

A leader's communications plan should include multiple elements of written and face-to-face connections planned to maximize the impact for the organization. Failure to communicate in good times and bad limits the effectiveness of the school leader, and it can lead to other things filling the void. This is when misinformation and rumors take root, and a community is fractured as a result.

Leaders owe it to themselves and those they are there to serve to provide effective, strategic, and meaningful updates on a consistent and ongoing basis. That's communication at its best!

LEADERSHIP POINTS TO REMEMBER REGARDING COMMUNICATION:

1. A leader needs to be specific and strategic with communication to his or her team.
2. A school leader needs to remember that e-mail is intended to share short, specific, and relevant information. Longer conversations and explanations should be shared face to face, on the phone, or in group settings.
3. Parents desire a personal connection with their school leader, and social media provides that opportunity. Individual leaders can identify the boundaries of what to share and when.

4. School leaders need to review their communication practices and include elements that build trust and value with their team.
5. A school leader should create avenues for students, parents, and team members to share recommendations and commendations.

FIVE

People and Praise: Encouragement Works

"Correction does much, but encouragement does more." —Johann Wolfgang
von Goethe, German writer, author, and politician

All school employees have their jobs because they are there to support students and parents. Without students and parents, these individuals would be unemployed or working in another industry or profession.

Parents interact with schools desiring exceptional academic experiences for their children. Students attend schools to interact and gain empowerment through participation in exceptional educational experiences.

So to ensure that school employees meet the expectations of those students and parents, it is essential that a leader be focused on their number one priority: people.

School leaders have a role to play with ongoing support, coaching, and encouragement of all team members in their care and employment. A leader has an obligation to focus on individuals to make certain that they are serving to their potential while helping identify areas of strength and future growth opportunities.

In a workforce hired to promote and achieve academic success, it is essential that leaders make the investment individually into employees, knowing that their success is directly tied to the school's success.

On every school campus, students, parents, and team members are quick to share with a leader which employees are their favorites, who is making an impact, and who is not working to their greatest potential. A leader should not be surprised by this feedback, but rather welcome having a community that is open and honest in sharing their recommendations and commendations when it comes to the human resource element of the school program.

A leader who values feedback and assessment of the workforce communicates the importance he or she places on parent and student comments in the evaluation of individual team members.

ESSENTIAL ENCOURAGEMENT PROOF POINTS

A healthy school community should take into account, and place a high value on, parent and student satisfaction with the educational program and its workforce.

As a charter school leader, you should be soliciting feedback from time to time in different public and private settings to gauge the effectiveness of programs, events, and people. Having this information will allow you to personally assess those on your team who may need coaching, feedback, and encouragement to increase their individual productivity and contributions to the team.

Employee evaluations should not be reserved to a one-time annual event, but rather, you should support employees with continuous and regular feedback on their performance. School leaders should focus on identifying three team members annually who need to be coached to increase their productivity and job satisfaction. That satisfaction should not come at the cost of compromising student learning.

A nominal teacher is a priority for all school leaders. When a teacher working with students is not maximizing a positive educational experience that is sustainable and long lasting, student learning is compromised and academic outcomes suffer. Leaders have an obligation to coach these teachers directly and aggressively, knowing that students shouldn't miss out on content or repeat a year of learning based on the ineffectiveness of an instructor.

Leaders in this situation should be in these classrooms regularly to monitor content delivery, instructional practices, and connection to individual students along the academic continuum from struggling to gifted. Just as a team of educators would meet with a student who was experiencing challenges to improve performance, a leader should also be pulling in personnel and resources to help a struggling teacher improve.

Teachers and leaders need to act as a team to focus on improvement so that each classroom environment is a place of encouragement, enrichment, and empowerment for all students to achieve.

Now that a leader knows that an investment of time and training needs to be made with these three individuals, he or she must not lose sight of supporting the rest of the school team as well.

Exceptional leaders are honest and direct with teachers they have identified for coaching and improvement. These individuals need to hear and see that a leader's expectations for them are directly tied to what is best for the students in their care.

Teachers also need to know the plan that has been established for their professional growth. Just telling someone they are being watched is not enough to dictate their professional improvement.

A school leader should have a plan in place before identifying and approaching employees for coaching and improvement. Employees will need to know that there are specific and measurable items that will be reviewed and targeted for improvement.

Here is a simple performance measure that can be used as a guide in developing your own coaching plan for individual employees.

1. Establish performance goal(s).
2. This evaluation period is a great time to define the individual goals that you have for these employees. It is unlikely that your three teachers will share the same improvement areas, so be specific with the three to five goals you have for these employees.

   Undefined expectations will not lead to growth and improvement. If anything, the situation will get worse without establishing specific and meaningful parameters and encouragement tied to established goals and objectives for their individual professional growth and success.
3. Define expectations of excellence.
4. With your leadership, it is imperative that you define the nature, culture, and value of the enriching classroom environment you wish to see at your school site. Teachers are very creative by nature, and with some specific guidelines and feedback, a leader can establish the parameters by which all instructional delivery is centered for maximum impact for student learning.

   This approach does not take away from a teacher's individual creativity, but rather allows him or her to focus individual skills and abilities on lesson planning. By standardizing the format and guidelines, the teacher is able to maximize his or her impact on the students in his or her care.
5. Schedule instructional visits.
6. Teachers being coached in order to improve their performance need to have a specific calendar of times when a leader will be present so that they can plan accordingly. This is not to say that the leader cannot deviate from that calendar, but being consistent with classroom observations sets a standard that this activity is a priority for the leader in helping this teacher succeed.

   It is hard to hold a teacher accountable for outcomes if a leader is not placing a priority on consistent and specific visitation dates and times.
7. Monitor individual progress.
8. A leader should provide notes and face-to-face feedback after each classroom observation. Giving the teacher specific examples of suc-

cess and areas where he or she still needs to develop is essential to the improvement plan for the employee.

A leader's encouragement will be crucial in helping move these employees from good to great. Plus, having these notes available to review at each meeting will showcase where the teacher has improved or areas of concern that still need specific attention.

Remember, everyone needs constructive criticism to grow and improve in his or her role. Just having a credentialed teacher certificate doesn't guarantee someone is a great teacher. Encouragement, praise, and honest assessment from a leader moves that teacher from "needs improvement" to "most improved."

9. Review professional accomplishments.
10. Based on the number of classroom visits and instructional sessions a leader has attended to observe the teacher, a summary of success should be created and shared with the employee. Along with that summary, action items should be included that will become the follow-up professional development agenda for the employee.

    As a leader, you should make an effort to provide a resource or tool for each of those listed action items. Do not expect that just because they are listed the employee will know how to address and strengthen performance in these areas. Your encouragement in linking support to needed improvement is a way to align expectations with available resources that the teacher can use to enhance his or her skills.
11. Make future plans.
12. Now that a leader has moved into a coaching role with specific employees, by mid-school year a determination will have to be made regarding future planning and hiring decisions for the coming school year. School leaders are usually focused on future programming, events, and activities six months out, if not more.

    Personnel decisions are also on this same timeline, and leaders must review the outcomes of their coaching and make a decision that is in the best interest of students. Knowing that some teachers will improve with direct feedback, while others will not, you must be courageous and decisive with all employment decisions.

    Remember that schools are not employment agencies, and not everyone gets to keep their job year after year without measurable and specific improvement.

A leader's work in the coaching arena with specific teachers annually is a priority to ensure that the team of educators is improving professionally to directly benefit students in their care. Students should have an expectation that each of their instructors is passionate, effective, and knowledgeable in their content area. Students should not be subjected to a teacher that is nominal, unskilled, or unprofessional.

A leader's tool kit should include encouragement, praise, and recognition as a means to inspire, harness, and connect learning and improved outcomes for all teachers, including those being coached to improve their performance.

LEADER-DRIVEN RECOGNITION AND ENCOURAGEMENT

As a school leader, the focus on encouraging a team should include opportunities to showcase individual contributions while rewarding excellence and promoting a culture of praise. An employee's hard work and positive impact should be celebrated and rewarded. Employees who set an example of excellence should be recognized for the value they bring to the organization, and for the students and parents they serve.

Recognition is an area that doesn't require a lot of work, but it does require that a leader take notice, value, and appreciate areas of excellence that are worth recognizing in his or her workforce. If leaders want to see increased job satisfaction with their employees, here are a few steps that lead to increased productivity.

1. Recognize publicly what you value personally.

This is a great way of setting a culture of praise and encouragement. If you want employees to arrive on time daily, reward that behavior. This can be as simple as mentioning publicly your appreciation for those employees by name at a team meeting. Make a point to praise publicly so that all team members know the value you place on their timeliness.

This same practice can be used for a multitude of topics that range from timeliness, to organizational skills, to the leadership demonstrated on a team or individual project. If you are a leader who utilizes technology to communicate a weekly message to your team, consider mentioning specific employees and their contributions to the organization in your update.

2. Recognize privately what you value personally.

It is also a great idea to write a personal note from time to time to all of the employees. A birthday, holiday, or special occasion seems like the obvious time to accomplish this task. However, a leader should also regularly target team members who are making an impact to receive a personal note of thanks or congratulations.

The handwritten message should be specific and speak to a character trait or a job accomplished that benefits the team and those whom you serve. If a teacher did a great presentation at a staff meeting, write a personal note of thanks to detail the elements that connected with the team. If the receptionist handled a difficult situation or an angry parent effectively, write a personal note and praise him or her for staying cool and calm in a difficult situation.

If a teacher created a great academic activity that engaged and inspired students, write a note of thanks to detail your praise of the elements that caught your personal attention.

Taking a few minutes to provide a simple handwritten, personal note to individuals on your team translates into building a strong personal connection between you and members of your workforce. Individual and specific praise is a very effective leadership tool that should be used often and unsparingly to benefit the employee and the organization.

Most e-mail programs offer a send later feature that can be used by the leader to draft notes to team members that will arrive days or weeks later to coincide with a special event or the employee's participation at a school event or activity. This is a great way for a leader to utilize technology to recognize individual accomplishments by those on his or her team.

A culture of encouragement and praise is built when a leader takes the time to value team members through acts of kindness shared in written and face-to-face meetings with individual employees.

3. Recognize employees with awards and events.

Encouragement and recognition for employees can also come by having a leader create and host an awards celebration for employees annually. This is a low-cost and high-impact way to celebrate individuals and reward excellence on the team.

It is easy to create awards based on themes you value or want to instill in your team: Great Customer Service, Innovative Programming, Great Communicator or Collaborator, and Most Organized and Timely.

Another idea is gathering feedback from the entire team to have them pick the best employees who exhibit excellent behavior in a range of valued areas. Honors for the best teacher, best classified employee, and best overall employee are awards that inspire and connect with most employees. At The Classical Academies, we use our end-of-the-year gathering to honor such employees, and each individual recognized receives a tangible gift in recognition of his or her specific contribution to the team.

Having the team participate in giving feedback allows everyone to celebrate the best of the best. When colleagues participate in choosing and honoring their colleagues, it strengthens the impact of the award. This removes any doubt the team may have that a leader might be playing favorites by personally selecting award winners. Having the team involved in the awards process creates ownership and allows feedback in the creation of new awards and employee recognition.

If cost is a factor in determining whether or not to host an awards event for employees, a leader can easily create and give out simple certificates denoting specific awards and special recognition. Giving out small denominations of gift cards to specialty stores and restaurants is another much appreciated reward program for employees.

Since leaders control an employee's schedule, another creative idea is to reward an employee with a free afternoon or day off as a prize. Each of these ideas can be easily implemented with some time and consideration—and a leader will come to know which incentive is most valued by which employee. Once this is known, the impact of the recognition is amplified as employees value their manager for personally knowing their specific likes and dislikes.

Remember, your personal connection to your team members builds trust and strengthens communication within the organization.

These cost-effective incentive ideas, accompanied by a leader's sincerity, can be powerful tools that impact a team in a deep and meaningful way. Theodore Roosevelt was right when he said, "People don't care how much you know until they know how much you care."

Making small investments into employee incentives and recognition programs lets employees know how much their leader cares about them and their professional behavior.

4. Recognize your employees through other organizations.

Another way that a leader can encourage and recognize his or her best team members annually is to identify local organizations that host recognition and awards programs. Local chambers of commerce, foundations, and business organizations routinely host events honoring individuals from a number of industries, including education.

Based on these programs, a school leader can submit employee names from his or her team to be nominees at the event. This is a simple way to have employees honored while also receiving recognition for the school or organization. Employees feel grateful to have their names aligned with a public event that elevates them in the community outside their specific school.

These award events are usually held after school or in the evening. Accompanying his or her leader to an event where the employee will be honored is extremely meaningful. The venue, opportunity to network with other professionals, and individual recognition also elevate the employee in a way that an on-campus event with peers cannot attain. Community recognition for an employee is special and creates a unique and lasting impression, often leading to enhanced job satisfaction and motivation.

Now that you have identified local recognition events to help honor the best of the best on your campus, there are also regional and statewide programs that are available to provide your employees additional recognition and exposure for the positive impact they are having at your school. For instance:

Does your county office of education offer a recognition program that your school can connect to and participate in?

Does your state have a public charter school association that hosts an annual awards program that accepts nominations?

Does your state have other support organizations that honor school employees and successful programs?

These are ways to elevate your team, or individuals on your team, and strengthen their individual commitment to the organization in the process.

Once employees know that when they work hard and make a positive impact, their efforts will be recognized and rewarded, they are often more likely to invest more deeply in the program. An employee's passion is directly connected to the encouragement and acknowledgment he or she consistently receives from students, parents, colleagues, and the school leader.

5. Recognize your employees through parent and student feedback.

Parent and student satisfaction is the lifeblood of every public charter school. If they are pleased with a program, they are quick to share their thoughts with others in their scope of influence. The same can be said when they are not pleased with a program; they are quick to share that information, too. Collecting feedback from parents and students is one thing, but what you do with that feedback is another.

The impact of soliciting and collecting feedback from parents and students attending the program, as it relates to your team, can be a powerful experience. This feedback can be collected as part of the annual parent satisfaction survey or through a special request sent to parents by the school leader.

For elementary schools, parents should be encouraged to provide feedback about all employees. At the high school level, students and parents should be encouraged to provide feedback about employees with whom they interact. Establishing a process to collect parent and student comments is another form of encouragement and praise that can be used to inspire and motivate your team members.

Now that a leader has started acknowledging his or her team on a consistent basis, another great idea is to place individual employee names in a jar for the number of times they are thanked or praised for a job well done. Once a month a drawing is held for that favored parking place, an afternoon off, or a certificate to sleep in late. This simple recognition program honors individuals and provides leaders with incentives that drive productivity within the workforce.

EMPLOYEE-DRIVEN RECOGNITION AND PRAISE

Now that a leader-driven recognition and encouragement program has been started, it is time to move to phase two, by having employees participate in recognizing and encouraging one another. At The Classical Academies, we encourage employees who see another team member acting in a manner that deserves acknowledgment to send an e-mail, copy the leader, and share the reason that individual is being praised for a job well done.

The leader, in turn, might add that employee's name to the mix, putting him or her in the running for the monthly reward. The site leader cannot be present to witness each employee making good decisions. Asking the team to recognize and share each other's hard work helps to make sure the visible and invisible accomplishments are acknowledged.

The actions of having employees praise one another drives home the point that individual actions in the workplace matter and are valued by all. There is always increased value in having a workforce that is keeping one another accountable by recognizing the best in each other. When is the last time you yourself didn't enjoy hearing from someone else about what you did well, that what you accomplished was noteworthy, and that your actions positively impacted the team or organization?

Praising people is valuable, and having all levels of the organization involved when it comes to recognition and encouragement makes a real difference.

COMMUNITY SUPPORT FOR EMPLOYEE RECOGNITION AND AWARDS

In public education, especially charter school education, there are limited dollars to pour into recognition and award programs. Sometimes leaders can be hard pressed to utilize even the smallest of amounts, even though they know this can make a great impact on employees. This is why a leader from time to time should look to the business community for support with organizational efforts to recognize individual accomplishments.

Think of all the places you interact with weekly as a consumer. Now process the benefit of simply asking for their support in providing a donation of goods and services to your public school to use to reward your hardworking employees. What's the worst they can say? No! It is not hard to compute the value of your patronage weekly to a business, so as a leader, leverage this information to help motivate the store or business owner.

For example, you can begin by saying something like, "I have been shopping at this store for a number of years and enjoy the products and services you provide. I am a faithful customer of yours, and I plan to shop here for several more years as you are close to my home or workplace. I am a public school leader and am collecting donations of goods and services from local businesses that I support to reward my hardworking employees. How can you help me in this effort?" With each of your dedicated employees in mind, making this request of a local business owner should come easily, knowing that your efforts will be greatly appreciated in the end.

These requests can easily be accomplished by sending an e-mail or letter request from time to time throughout the school year. If a leader is fortunate enough to have parent volunteers available, this is a good project to assign, knowing that parents value helping support an exceptional school team. Plus, if you have parents that work at local businesses and organizations, they are very likely open to making the request of their employers on a leader's behalf.

Some national businesses have a giving or charitable arm and are looking for local nonprofits and schools annually to help support, so spend some time researching these areas for assistance, too.

Targeting businesses annually with donation requests is usually the best way to gain their support, as it is a good reminder about the school and the ongoing need for community support. Asking too frequently can lead a business owner or organization to feel like the school is taking advantage of their generosity.

Developing private-sector relationships is never a waste of time; rather, it provides the ability for a leader to make connections in the community for the benefit of the students, parents, and school employees. These relationships lead to financial support as well as local advocacy.

A leader's job is to be bold in supporting his or her employees. Personally asking businesses to assist a school is a courageous move that brings rewards and benefits to a hardworking school team. Whether through private investment with goods and services or school recognition programs, be sure to emphasize the importance of people serving in your organization. Encouragement really does work wonders for people, including those who spend lots of their time and energy encouraging the students in their care.

LEADERSHIP POINTS TO REMEMBER
REGARDING PEOPLE AND PRAISE:

1. Employee evaluations should not be reserved as an annual event; support employees with continuous feedback on their performance.
2. A school leader should have a plan in place before identifying and approaching employees for coaching and improvement. Identify specific and measurable items that will be reviewed and targeted for improvement.
3. A leader's handwritten message of praise should be specific and speak to a character trait or a job accomplished that benefits the team and patron. It should be used often and unsparingly to benefit the employee and the organization.
4. A culture of encouragement and praise is built when a leader takes the time to value team members through acts of kindness shared in written and face-to-face meetings.
5. The action of having employees praise one another reinforces to the team that individual actions in the workplace matter and are valued by all. Keeping one another accountable by recognizing the best in each other is valuable.

SIX

So You Want to Be a
Charter School Leader!

"Leadership and learning are indispensable to each other." —President John
F. Kennedy

So are you ready? Is this crazy, mad charter school leadership ride for
you? Maybe you are currently occupying the charter school leadership
chair and chose this book for some encouragement and a reminder that
you are on the right track with your students, your parents, and your
charter school colleagues.

Maybe you are one of those talented professionals who is looking to
get into the charter school leadership game to enjoy all the challenges and
successes of helping create a sustainable and relevant program that connects learning to life for students.

Either way, seasoned school leader or novice, I wrote this book for
you.

As you have read in the previous chapters, the job of charter school
leadership is not for everyone and requires a skill set that is unique,
varied, and diversified. Great schools are managed by a select few who
are able to harness the elements required for success and make them
applicable at their school site for the betterment of students.

There is not a one size fits all when it comes to charter school leadership. Success is not gender based, and men and women share equally in
the potential impact. An ability to adapt, align, and stay in tune with
student needs and parent expectations is crucial. A leader who provides a
workplace that is progressive and relevant for an educational professional to feel needed and valued is truly a prized commodity.

Charter school leadership is a profession that takes passion, vision,
and a personal sense of ownership. Leaders who personalize their role

and believe, "This is my school. These are my students. These are my parents," are driven by a commitment to excellence in meeting the needs of the entire school community.

These individuals are the flag bearers for parent school choice in communities all across America. These are the leaders who are making a difference daily in public education by managing highly effective public charter schools.

DIFFERING BACKGROUNDS IN LEADERSHIP

Charter school leadership holds a unique place in the public school arena. This position is filled with educators, businessmen and businesswomen, scholars, entrepreneurs, and general risk takers. Many of these individuals have placed their faith, personal savings, and reputations on the line to open a school for the benefit of the community. These individuals stand alone in their communities by taking a dream, detailed in the founding charter school documents, and then attaching people, process, and policies to form a living, breathing educational community.

Charter school leaders often eclipse their traditional school counterparts in business sense by having a firsthand working knowledge of what it takes to create, organize, and manage all elements of an organization. These charter school leaders have to manage all these areas so that schools can open—and stay open.

In some cases, these charter school leaders manage multiple schools with enrollments that surpass the size of some smaller public school districts. This in itself requires a leader who appreciates and understands the fundamentals and infrastructure of what it takes to manage and maintain a school or large organization.

Not many traditional school superintendents can claim the scars or victories that come from opening a new school, let alone starting a business from scratch. The business of running a charter school clearly requires an expanded skill set not often found in traditional school district offices.

A traditional superintendent has most likely grown up within the traditional school district. Once a classroom teacher, then a principal, this individual worked as an assistant superintendent before being selected as a superintendent to oversee the district and its schools. These men and women understand and work within a decades-old system and are expected to maintain the organization with limited changes.

Few superintendents take on the risk of implementing the sweeping change needed in most public school districts, knowing that these moves will come at a high price—sometimes their jobs. Union leaders and traditional thinkers inside the public school system often oppose systematic, sustainable, and widespread change to business as usual.

Consider Washington, D.C.'s school chancellor, Michelle Rhee, as an example of someone who chose to make drastic changes to her school district, and the backlash that came as a result. Ms. Rhee's focused and strategic approach to reforming her schools, teacher contracts, and spending priorities brought great controversy and raised the public discourse on funding failing schools.

Charter school leaders and public school reformers applaud her efforts and view the work she was accomplishing as the first step needed in championing the cause of returning the national conversation to strengthening, changing, and innovating public education. Ms. Rhee and others drew a line in the sand saying, "Enough is enough"—it was time to put the needs of students first.

Charter school leaders often have to push traditional boundaries and leave the status quo behind, ensuring that academic needs of students are addressed with individualized and personalized approaches to learning. Gone are the days when one size fits all in public education. Gone are the days when one book, one lecture, one classroom meet the needs of all in attendance.

The national trend is now looking at personalized learning as a means to connect, inspire, and academically challenge students to excel. Charter school leaders are required to continually look at innovative educational approaches to ensure that students are academically challenged and their teams of educators are effective and progressive in meeting those student needs.

With the push to innovate, reorganize, and reinvent public education, charter school leaders urge continual review of content, delivery, and instructional practices to improve their schools from year to year. How a charter school opened and performed five or ten years ago only matters when reviewing historical data.

A charter school leader should always evaluate current trends and not rely on past success to gauge and plan for the future. Most successful leaders review data and trends from students and parents. Based on this information, leaders annually make adjustments to the charter school program to maximize continuous and measurable improvement.

Charter schools that open and quickly find success based on academic standings and parent satisfaction rarely find themselves in the same position a decade later without making adjustments to their program. The landscape of public education is continually changing. These landscape modifications are not only based on the demographics of the school's student population, but they also develop according to technology, content standards, and educational research into best practices.

These shifts in the educational landscape demand that a charter school leader keep an eye on what is changing so that his or her school remains a relevant academic program meeting the needs of students.

Charter schools that continue business as usual will find the relevance of their programs fading as parents are continually seeking high-quality options for their student's education. If a leader fails to exercise leadership in making strategic modifications to his or her program, a great charter school runs the risk of slipping to good. In education, students, parents, and the community shouldn't have to settle for a good school. A charter school leader wants to give his or her community a great school.

Charter school laws vary from state to state. A great school in one state may not be found with that same format or educational philosophy in another state, or another school. Some flourishing school models have bridged the gap and have successfully replicated their school business model within the community, region, state, or nation. These programs are usually overseen by a charter management organization, or CMO.

Individual schools within the CMO group maintain their individual school integrity by being managed from the top, or from one central location. This process allows for all schools to maintain the culture, business operations, staff development, and training needed to keep these schools in tune and aligned with the stated mission and vision of their charter, no matter what state or community they may be located in.

Maintaining a CMO model can prove an operational challenge for a school leader, and as such, the governing board for an individual school will have to determine if and when to open the door to creating a CMO that will manage multiple schools under one leadership model.

Once that management decision is made to open a second, third, or fourth school, it is key that the charter school leader develops a succession and management plan. This plan's focus is to ensure that culture, academic programming, and organizational integrity is maintained at all levels of the organization. Having this plan in place limits the impact felt if and when there is a leadership change.

TRAINING THE NEXT WAVE OF LEADERS

In the development of a leadership training program, it is best for the current charter school leader to identify specific elements that make the school a unique place for learning and fundamental elements that he or she wants to instill in and pass on to those individuals being trained for future leadership opportunities within the organization.

The common areas that all school leaders should consider covering in their leadership program can be easily aligned to any specific school or group of schools.

Leadership Styles and Their Impact

What type or style is valued within the organization?

A charter school leader should be in tune with the leadership style he or she has and values. Having this information will allow the leader to define in word and deed what is expected from all incoming team members and leaders—the style that is used to form and sustain the charter school program.

This is not to say that all future leaders need to act and facilitate in the exact same manner to secure a position within the organization, but all leaders need to have an overview and appreciation of leadership styles to understand their own and the possible impact they will have as a result.

Some applicants for charter school leadership have gained personal knowledge of management hierarchy by the simple virtue of having worked in several jobs before finding employment in the education field. Even with that, some individuals will be new to the public charter school arena, and as such, some may have never experienced entrepreneurial ideas and the changes they bring to traditional school leadership positions.

Having individuals with a willingness and openness to consider new leadership ideas will be necessary as these employees move into charter school leadership positions. A well-rounded and flexible individual will make the transition to leader more easily, and the school and community will benefit.

Today's charter school leaders must be able to articulate their leadership styles so they can set the stage for training all new leaders. While knowing that everyone is unique and brings a different set of personal and professional experiences to the table, the current leader should never appoint a new leader who is not in alignment with the current leadership style, elements, or traits.

To do so will divide the team, or worse yet, impact the learning community and the established, expected school-wide academic outcomes. Making strategic management decisions must be a priority for every leader when determining the next line of leaders for the organization. Delegating this responsibility would be the wrong approach; these hiring decisions will have a lasting impact on the school's future.

Customer Service and Expectations

What do you want the team to understand and value as an organization?

Customer service is an essential element in the success of a charter school program. As new schools are established and parents from the traditional school settings begin to make contact with these new schools, customer service is critical in helping parents connect with a particular program.

Most traditional school parents have an established expectation for dealing with a school. It is the job of the charter school leader and his or her professional school team to exceed that parent expectation. That can happen by being committed to a few customer service ground rules that are established and maintained by every charter school employee consistently.

- An employee and not a voicemail answering service will answer all incoming telephone calls.
- All e-mails will be responded to within 24 hours, if not sooner.
- All leaders will respond to parent e-mails with a telephone call on all matters of importance.
- All leaders will be available and visible during student drop-off and pick-up times at the start and completion of the school day to be accessible to parents.
- All school employees, especially those with direct contact with students and parents, will maintain a friendly and approachable manner at all times.

These are just a few of the customer service elements that a leader should focus on with all employees seeking a leadership position within the organization. Charter school leaders taking personal ownership of these elements will set the expectations and personally influence those in their workplace.

Providing excellent service to students, parents, and fellow colleagues is an area where all schools can look to make improvements. Hosting regular conversations on these topics at meetings and gatherings with students, parents, and charter school professionals will keep the focus on what is valued and expected when it comes to providing excellent customer service and exceeding parent expectations.

Workplace Corporate Culture

What ideals and values are desired to promote alignment within the workforce to keep all in tune with leadership expectations?

Creating, impacting, and sustaining a workplace corporate culture is paramount to a leader's lasting impact on the charter school program. There is a plethora of information available on the importance of creating a corporate culture and its value to nurturing a school committed to academic and social success of students. What is not readily available is the step-by-step process to make it happen.

As Drs. Steve and Rebecca Wilke share in their book *Corporate Family Matters*, culture is comprised of three essential components: values, beliefs, and behavior patterns. They explain that exceptional leaders must define the culture of their organization first, then they should cascade its tenets to every member on their team.

If culture isn't defined, then everything from disorganization to corporate chaos can occur. Organizations with strong cultures are the ones that not only survive, but also tend to thrive. This is true in every profession—including the business of education.

Leaders of new charter schools will be able to help create and develop the original culture of the school, while those who take on a leadership position in an existing school will discover a culture already in place.

In either case, the elements of that culture must be intentionally developed and then passed on to all team members on a regular, consistent basis. This takes time and effort, but the value of keeping the culture thriving will be seen in the overall impact the school's program has on students.

Character Education

What do character-driven school leaders expect?

Many traditional public and charter schools have an adopted character education program to help promote valuable traits of honesty, integrity, and responsibility among students attending the program. A school leader should also have his or her leadership embrace those same character education elements.

With this educational focus happening on campus for the students, coupled with leaders also actively embracing these concepts, this process brings the school culture into alignment as everyone is valuing and striving to be character driven in their daily activities and interactions.

Additional value comes when the school leader begins to recognize and reward behavior of students and employees that aligns with the character education program in an active and meaningful way. This showcases publicly what is valued on campus by the leader, not only for students, but also for the adults connected with the program internally and externally.

When parents begin to see regular updates from the school community that include a student and employee recognition program based on the established character education program, they begin to feel a sense of pride knowing that the charter school leader is valuing and rewarding behaviors that are grounded in elements that are being taught and modeled for their students.

A school leader should review character education programs closely and look for those that can be embraced personally, as well as for students, parents, and his or her charter school colleagues. At The Classical Academies, we utilize *8 Keys of Excellence*—distributed by Learning Forum International, a 501(c)(3) nonprofit educational corporation based in Oceanside, California— as our character education program.

Business 101

What are the elements needed for leaders to understand managing the business side of the charter school organization?

Many who have chosen educational leadership as a career start as classroom teachers. They spend their days interacting with students, creating lesson plans, and communicating with parents. Within a few years, some of these teachers may have a desire to move into school leadership and find themselves as assistant or school principals. Even in these traditional school roles, employees are not immersed in the business of running an organization.

Having a charter school leadership program that covers some of the basic elements of accounting, budgeting, human resources, benefits, payroll, and retirement reporting allows emerging leaders to have a better understanding of the charter school organization. The charter school is in place to educate students, but a charter school leader also needs to understand that there is an infrastructure to manage beyond just that of a solid academic program.

ORGANIZATIONAL SUPPORT FOR LEADERS

Charter school leaders need to become familiar with the state and national organizations that are in place to support individual charter schools. Many advocacy and charter school support organizations are designed and managed by educational reformers committed to working for the betterment of public education by developing membership organizations to benefit charter schools.

These organizations vary in prominence and influence from state to state. Those states with fewer numbers of charter schools may find themselves drawn to national or larger state organizations for resources and information on best practices and advocacy information to help their individual charter school.

Various charter school membership and support organizations can easily be found through a quick Internet search or by obtaining a referral from an existing charter school leader operating a successful school.

Many of these organizations do offer free services to new leaders wanting to start a charter school, or they will provide information needed to manage a successful public charter school. Receiving wise legal, financial, and organizational advice and explanations is vital to a new school's successful launch and, upon joining these advocacy groups, a school gains access to a vast amount of experience and knowledge.

Access to a state or nationally staffed legal team or financial advisors, for instance, is paramount to a smooth and successful opening of a new school. With the volume of resistance and protest to the creation of charter schools, advice from these groups helps to prevent new charter schools from being closed on technical issues.

In the state of California, there are two prominent and successful charter school advocacy organizations available to help emerging or seasoned school leaders open their doors and keep them open.

The California Charter Schools Association (CCSA) has a regional presence throughout the state and offers free and membership-based tools and resources to help new — and seasoned — leaders along a path to success. This organization is fully engaged in helping students, parents, school employees, and school leaders play an active and meaningful role in the school choice movement statewide. Their work is being recognized nationally as the largest statewide charter school membership organization.

The Charter Schools Development Center (CSDC) is the oldest and most trusted charter school membership and support organization in California. Its director, Eric Premack, was involved in the formation of the California Charter Schools Act legislation that became law in 1992. Since that time, CSDC and Mr. Premack have maintained an active and prominent position at the state level to ensure that state policy and lawmakers on a continual basis hear a founding voice for the movement of public school choice in California. Mr. Premack has personally championed the freedoms of students and parents since 1992, and his policy work will continue to have a lasting impact on public education for decades to come.

These two organizations are merely examples of the premium quality options that are available to charter school leaders in California looking for support in managing their charter school or charter school organization.

For those states with public charter schools, the state's department of education will most likely have an office or individual assigned to support or provide information on charter school programming and alternative school options. A school leader should maintain an awareness of and personal connection to this office or individual appointed to oversee charter schools.

It is a good practice for a charter school leader to schedule a meeting with this key individual or department to showcase his or her school, its academic outcomes, and the elements of success unique to his or her charter school program. A leader should welcome opportunities to share with state officials and gain a better knowledge of how these individuals and departments can benefit his or her school. It is always a welcome surprise to locate new resources and information to help benefit your students, parents, and charter school program.

A leader should not make the mistake of thinking that state employees or state departments have an active and current awareness of specific charter school programs. A charter leader taking the time to schedule a meeting with state officials about his or her school from time to time is time well spent.

By making state or regional connections, charter school leaders can gain support for the students and parents within the learning community. There is valuable information shared during these gatherings, and a discussion about the successes and failures helps everyone in the charter world. These meetings and connections greatly benefit the school when state leaders are looking for specific examples of innovative programming and successful school models to visit or showcase.

As a charter school leader communicating your school-wide learning results in the form of a newsletter or general update, consider the value of sending this same publication to state and local leaders to keep them informed about your school or schools. This is a simple way to maintain contact with interested parties while continuing to spread the news regarding the school's value and impact on the public education landscape in your community.

Some national support organizations for charter school leaders include:

Center for Education Reform

   910 Seventeenth Street, NW
   11th Floor
   Washington, DC 20006
   Telephone: 800-521-2118
   www.edreform.com

National Alliance for Public Charter Schools

   1101 15th Street, NW
   Suite 1010
   Washington, DC 20005
   Telephone: 202-289-2700
   Fax: 202-289-4009
   www.publiccharters.org

National Charter School Resource Center

   c/o American Institutes for Research
   1000 Thomas Jefferson Street, NW
   Washington, DC 20007-3835
   Telephone: 877-277-2744
   Fax: 202-403-6222
   www.charterschoolcenter.org

Each of these agencies is a great place to locate statistics, publications, and information on charter schools and their best practices. These agencies, along with individual state charter school support organizations, are also a resource to share with parents and interested members of the community wanting more information on charter schools, their impact, and their success.

All of these organizations share the goal of educating the community at large on the value and sustainability of charter schools and their place in public education.

For many charter school leaders, just knowing that these agencies and organizations are committed to public awareness allows them to focus in on their individual school, while leaving the larger picture of the school reform movement in the organizations' capable hands. These charter school leaders know that, if and when parents or community members want or desire more in-depth information on the school choice movement, they have these agencies to turn to in helping tell that story with additional facts and information.

Charter school leaders are well served when they provide links to agencies and organizations that support charter schools on their school's website for parents and the community to easily access. This is a simple way for an individual school to connect others to the larger school reform movement nationally. Too often, students, parents, and charter school professionals forget that they are part of a national educational trend impacting millions.

As covered in a previous chapter on communications, a great way to boost a school's social media dialogue online is to supplement your school's postings with national information, reports, and success stories supplied by these agencies and organizations. Posting national statistics from time to time reminds your community of the impact your school is helping to create that feeds into the national picture of school reform.

National organizations also host meetings, seminars, webinars, and conferences as a way to connect charter school leaders to training, information sharing, and networking opportunities. These resources are helpful not only in connecting leaders, but also in gathering data shared by individual leaders about their schools. This data collection builds a picture of the national impact being made as a collective of public charter schools.

With charter schools currently serving just less than 10 percent of public school students (K–12) nationally, the reputation of charter schools is strengthening with each year. There is still a relatively large segment of the public that is unaware that charter schools are indeed publicly funded and are public schools. This is an area where an effective charter school leader can make a difference locally by educating the community by being readily available to speak at service clubs and local business organizations about the national movement while highlighting his or her local school or schools.

Over the last two decades, charter schools have gotten a bad reputation because some have claimed that these schools are the panacea for the public school system. Charter school leaders will stress that these schools are merely educational models established to add to the academic options available in a community to help meet the needs of all students. They are not the solution to all of the challenges in the traditional school system. Options in public education are a benefit to students, parents, and the community.

Charter leaders will go on to detail that when the local school district recognizes and accepts the successes at neighboring charter schools, it will understand that these schools are bettering the educational landscape in their own communities. Ideally, this leads to implementation of innovation and change within their own traditional settings to benefit students.

Charter schools are often the testing grounds and the centers of innovation that allow communities to try new and unique programs and apply educational options to assist students with varied learning styles and abilities.

What is clear is that through the work of state and national charter school support agencies and organizations, the public's perception of charter schools is changing for the better. What makes a difference locally is having an effective charter school leader making positive gains for students while standing up to champion options in education that improve the landscape of public education for all.

These leaders continually refocus the discussion to the belief that education is all about the students and preparing them to be the leaders, now and into the future.

CHARTER SCHOOL SHARING AND COLLABORATION

Charter school leaders by nature come from a place of wanting to share and learn from others. They are open to new ideas and embrace collaboration and information sharing. For those leaders fortunate enough to operate their schools in close proximity to one or more charter schools, it is often the case that these leaders will get to know each other and welcome regularly scheduled meetings to discuss their challenges, successes, and ongoing opportunities for growth.

These kinds of meetings allow individual charter school leaders to find encouragement, common ground, and a sense of accomplishment by hearing from other leaders. After building trust and transparency with one another, these gatherings can be a place where information and ideas are exchanged while providing a time to reflect on past challenges and successes with colleagues.

These are the people who share your interests and who understand firsthand the pressures and challenges of being a charter school leader. They are in the trenches with you. Most likely they share your interests, your goals, and your fortitude. This places them in the perfect spot to provide you with professional feedback and give you a sounding board for information and ideas.

The year 2011 marked the 20th anniversary of the charter school movement in the United States, and there are many leaders of today's charter schools who have been in the movement for more than a decade. These leaders are looking for personal and professional staff development and training options that speak to their years of experience, giving them new information and challenging them to grow.

Having leaders connect and collaborate with fellow charter school leaders locally and regionally is an excellent way for these school leaders to find new information and resources. These are great opportunities to hear from other experts and learn firsthand how other leaders are finding success.

Collaboration and information sharing are critical for public schools to improve and innovate, always remaining progressive and relevant for the students and community they are there to serve. Charter school leaders owe it to themselves to seek meetings with other charter school leaders to problem solve, share best practices, and challenge their own thinking on what is educationally optimal for students.

Charter school leaders are focused clearly on detailing their educational mission, vision, and how they think that students best learn. As these leaders share and collaborate with one another, they must not fear losing their individual school success. Each and every charter school is separate and different. Each has different students, parents, employees, and community supporters. Each school will have its own culture. Leaders ought to gather to learn from one another.

Unlike the fast food giants who refuse to divulge their secret sauce recipes, charter school innovations and options are openly shared in these meetings. Having charter schools that look and run differently is key to the industry's success. No one school holds the corner on the market by being all things to all students.

One of the best ways a charter school leader can find encouragement and ongoing training is to look for opportunities to share his or her school's best practices. This can be accomplished locally by contacting the chamber of commerce, a service club, or a business support organization. These groups are regularly looking for speakers with relevant information to share. School success is directly tied to community economic development efforts, so these organizations and groups value what a school leader has to share.

Individuals and businesses looking to relocate into a community regularly inquire about the strength and impact of the local public school system. Families want great schools for their children to attend, and employers desire great schools so that they are able to attract and retain highly qualified employees. The charter school story is worth telling—and the value these schools bring to a community is immeasurable.

Strengthening and improving the educational landscape of a city, or county, benefits families and businesses as it directly ties into communities' economic development efforts. Strong schools with varied options available will draw families who desire a strong education for their children. Companies then can settle nearby, attracting a strong workforce. This circular connection between schools, families, and corporate presence ought to be carefully considered by any community development council.

Charter school leaders also need to be deliberate about presenting at regional, state, and national conferences. These opportunities give school leaders a chance not only to showcase the school's best practices but also to immerse themselves in occasions to be shoulder to shoulder with state and national charter school leaders. These are fantastic opportunities for a leader to be strategic with planning and to connect with individuals who are making impressive strides in public education.

The charter school industry is just entering its third decade, so many of the industry pioneers are still on the scene making a difference and welcome meeting with new leaders in the field. Sharing at a conference or state meeting gives any leader access to these early innovators in the charter school movement, and being able to ask questions directly of the original charter school innovators is often eye opening.

BECOMING A CHARTER SCHOOL LEADER

Now that I have detailed the elements needed to inspire your team and thrive as a charter school leader, you may be asking the simple question, "How do I become a charter school leader?"

For me, it started with a desire to become involved with helping start a charter school in my own community. My young family was searching for schooling options and carefully considered the opportunities available in traditional public, private, and charter public schools. You can do the same.

Here is a basic step-by-step process that numerous people have followed as they started their journey and have become outstanding leaders working daily to improve public education starting with their individual school.

Start With a Dream

There is a personal reason to start a charter school—what's yours?
What motivates you?
Why do you want to start a school?
What will your school look like?
What unique or special educational programming or elements will it include?
What population of students will it serve?
What is your philosophy of education?
How will this be applied to creating your charter school?

Who Do You Know?

Having connections is critical to getting your charter school approved.
Who do you—or some of your friends—know on the local school board?
What city or community leaders do you or your friends know?
Do you have any connections to your state legislators?
Who do you know that can make some telephone calls or schedule some meetings for you to meet influential people in your community?

A portfolio of personal references or letters that speak of your qualifications and can be attached to your charter school application lends credibility and strength to your petition to open a charter school. Not having these in hand can stop a charter school petition or application from even being considered by a local school board.

Check the Requirements

For those states with charter schools, the state's department of education will list the requirements that every charter school must detail in its application or founding charter document. The charter school developer will need to detail how his or her school will meet these required elements.

Most states have a copy of all the approved charter documents to date, and some make these available online for viewing. These are valuable in that others can read how each of these schools planned to meet its goals by detailing the school's mission, vision, how it believes students best learn, and how the individual school will uniquely address each of these elements.

It may be in the developer's best interest to contact a respected charter school, one that is making great academic gains, and ask for a copy of its charter to review. As a public agency, these documents are available to the general public.

Many schools make their charters available on their websites so anyone, including a new school developer, can view them. Once the new developer has investigated how other schools have written their charter applications, they can best determine in detail their plan to fulfill the state-mandated requirements for operation.

It is also a best practice to see if your state has a charter school support agency or organization to help start a new charter school. As described earlier, many host free or low-cost events for developers. Some of these agencies provide a template for the charter developers about what they should know. Some seasoned school boards prefer a template approach when reviewing a new school for approval.

This is where a developer's connections come into play.

What does your local school district want?

Does the local school board want a template or a creative, personal approach that has been crafted and created for your new school?

What extra information should a developer include with the submission that is not necessarily required by the state, but will be requested by the district?

Being well prepared in advance with this information can make the approval process easier and more manageable.

Established charter school leaders are usually open to a meeting with a new charter school developer to help provide advice and detail possible pitfalls they experienced previously in the development of their schools. These school leaders also have established relationships in the community that may be of benefit to you and your future school.

Don't be afraid to ask for these school leaders' help in making a connection or scheduling a meeting with someone who can help get your charter school approved. It's good to remember the motto, "It's not what you know but who you know."

Check on Funding

Does your state offer access to grant funding to start a charter school? This information is most likely found on the state's website, along with the charter school requirements and legislative information. If you cannot find it on the website, make a quick call to the state's contact on charter schools and ask.

Also, another easy option is to contact your charter school advocacy organization and ask about grants and possible incentives available to you as you plan and seek to open a new charter school.

Larger philanthropic organizations that give to charter schools are usually not open to personal inquiries for funding for a new school. Many of these programs are looking to support established and results-heavy programs with a track record of success. However, many developers are not deterred and find themselves calling some of the most popular organizations to inquire for themselves. It can never hurt to ask personally!

During the search for concrete funding, your connections to local charitable organizations will be a benefit. Do they fund educational opportunities in your community? If they do, what are the requirements to apply?

Developers will find that much of their time, money, and effort to open a new school are a personal investment. Funders love to join a successful party in progress, but few, if any, provide seed money to help get the party started.

Find Your Audience

Now that you have a school concept in place, and you want to seek city approval to open the school, the local school district will need to know that there is a need for your school in the community prior to granting that approval. Your great educational improvement idea is nothing without parents' interest and a strong desire to have their sons and daughters participate.

A school developer will need to collect signatures of interested parents as proof of interest—and as part of the charter school application process.

A developer should schedule a number of community meetings to detail the school concept to the general public. These meetings will feature a layout of the planned charter school programming and provide an opportunity for parents and community members to ask questions and gain a better understanding of how the charter school plans to add value to the public educational landscape and impact students enrolled.

These meetings can easily be promoted in the local newspaper as a free community event. One idea is to connect with a local community center, library, or church to locate some free space to host these community meetings. With each meeting, a developer is able to strengthen his or her presentation by including questions and information collected at the prior meetings.

At the conclusion of each informational meeting, a leader should request that interested parents sign the charter school petition that will be submitted for approval from the local school district, showcasing the community's need for this new school option. The collecting of an overabundance of signatures never guarantees a new school's approval.

Some school districts will invest the time in contacting everyone who signed the petition to inquire if they plan to send their children to this new school. Informing petitioners that this is a possibility helps equip them to know this call may be coming at some time in the charter review process by the school district.

Gauge the Environment for Approval

Now that you have collected your parent signatures and have some community support from parents, you ought to host meetings with local community leaders, the district superintendent, and some, if not all, of the elected school board members. These meetings will give you a sense of the community's willingness to approve a new charter school.

The charter author may have learned already through connections that there is openness to creating new school options in the community. Some superintendents embrace alternative school choices, knowing that these will help meet the academic needs of all students within his or her school district.

On the other hand, a developer may find he or she will face a major challenge in opening a new public charter school due to opinions held, and not easily changed, or established agendas that will prevent innovation and school choice under the current administration. A leader needs to remember that opening a new charter school does have political implications and that he or she should plan accordingly.

Understand the Appeals Process

If and when the charter petition is denied at the local school district level, it is important for the developer to understand the charter school appeal process. Some states have in place a system that will move the appeal from the district to the county office of education and then on to the state's board of education.

With these established processes, there are most likely state-mandated timelines for appeals. A charter school developer should be well versed in what his or her state requires—and know that this process may have to be utilized as a backup plan in the event that the charter school is denied at the local level.

Embrace and Appreciate the Workload

Once a charter school is approved, the real work begins. The checklist is long, and the charter school developer changes hats from developer to charter school leader. The prep work accomplished beforehand laid the groundwork for the charter school approval. Now approved, the new work begins immediately as the charter school leader has to bring life to the educational concept he or she advocated prior to approval.

Hiring employees, creating policies and procedures, locating facilities, and finding qualified and assertive individuals who are willing to serve on the school's board of directors are just a few priorities for a leader opening a new school.

The board of directors is chosen to provide oversight and accountability for the school leader and program. Charter school leaders should have an eye on whom they want on the school board, the expertise needed by each member, and the term of office defined as part of the charter school planning process. Once selected, these members and the established board cannot be easily changed.

There are multiple sources of information and publications on board development. One notable resource for charter school leaders is Brian L. Carpenter's 2009 book, *Charter School Board University: An Introduction to Effective Charter School Governance, Second Edition*. Since it is written specifically for charter schools, it is unique in its information and approach and will provide wise counsel for establishing a sound school board.

A school's business services need to be started as soon as people and processes are implemented. As a new employer, there are specific rules and regulations that must be followed and adhered to immediately. Much like any small business, the first two years are critical for a charter school. Over the last two decades, numerous charter schools have closed due to financial insolvency or a failed academic reputation.

A new charter school leader must have the professional wherewithal to know who to hire and when to hire. With the limited school funding available and its timed arrival from the state, it is necessary to coordinate all of this with the opening of the new school.

Charter school leaders must understand their own boundaries and skill sets to ensure that what they can accomplish actually happens, and a working board member completes what is still left to do as a volunteer. During the start-up phase, there are limited dollars to cover start-up costs. This is where a leader's passion and tenacity as well as his or her ability to think creatively come into play.

Enjoy the Ride

Charter school leaders need to "stop and smell the roses" from time to time. Many are so dedicated to their school's operation and success that they rarely, if ever, stop to take stock of their own success or accomplishments. Many workdays, endless nights, and numerous weekends pass with little recognition or praise.

These special leaders are making an ongoing personal sacrifice to see that their charter school is successful and sustainable. As one of these emerging leaders, it is important that you take time to appreciate the work being accomplished.

Don't forget to find joy in the work at hand and celebrate from time to time to remind yourself and others that what you are doing is important and meaningful. Your work is equipping and changing lives. Never forget that simple and meaningful truth.

Refuel and Replenish the Passion

A dedicated and passionate charter school leader is only as good as the balance he or she brings to the role. To maintain the leadership edge, individuals need a break from the work at hand from time to time. Valuing and appreciating "downtime" is essential for leaders to have long-lasting and sustainable success.

The amount of work required to get a new charter school up and running can be all consuming, and in the end, a leader's personal sacrifices will eventually impact other areas of his or her life. With all of the attention focused on the school and overall business operation, a leader can easily neglect other areas of life. One's personal life can temporarily lose some of its priority. This, if not checked, can easily become unbalanced and create a leader who is out of alignment with his or her personal obligations and responsibilities.

Charter school leaders need to count the cost and keep other priorities in sight to allow themselves to refuel and replenish their passion. One-sided leaders will limit their impact if they fail to schedule time for family, friends, hobbies, and other things they enjoy that are not work related.

A leader cannot undervalue the need for downtime and time for formulating new ideas and a fresh perspective, which only comes from stepping away from the work and resting.

A leader needs to schedule a break. Waiting for a day when there is nothing pressing will turn into weeks and months without a day off. Be purposeful about your time with family and friends, and by yourself.

Set a date for a vacation. Walk away from the office and the inbox. Once away, stay away. Turn off the smartphone. Turn off the e-mail arrival tone. Assertively and decisively avoid communications with your office, your co-workers, and your charter school community.

Your strategic and planned disconnect will benefit everyone: most importantly, you. Leadership is passionate work, and when done well, it is draining and creatively taxing.

If a leader desires to continually "be on their game," then breaks need to be scheduled and taken. A tired player is no use to the team. As such, a leader who is not fully engaged and fatigued is not good for the charter school or the organization.

So with all this new information, what's next for you?

Are you inspired to fill a leadership position that will benefit your charter school and the students whom you serve?

Are you ready to take on the task of starting a new charter school that will impact students' lives and your community and help change the educational landscape of public education?

I sure hope so! Your community needs your help. Parents need the public school options you will create and manage. Students want your new and innovative programs that inspire and equip them for college, career, and citizenship.

Ready—Set—Lead!

LEADERSHIP POINTS TO REMEMBER REGARDING BECOMING A CHARTER SCHOOL LEADER:

1. Charter school leadership is a profession that takes passion, vision, and a personal sense of ownership. Leaders who personalize their role are driven by a commitment to excellence.

2. Leaders should review data and trends from students and parents. Based on this information, adjustments can be made to the program to maximize continuous and measurable improvement.

3. A school leader should develop a secession and management plan focused on ensuring that culture, academic programming, and organizational integrity be maintained. Advanced planning limits the impact felt if and when there is a leadership change.

4. A charter school leader should be in tune with his or her leadership style. Understanding this will allow the leader to define in word and deed what is expected from all incoming team members and leaders.

5. Charter school leaders must seek and maintain a solid working relationship with key state officials or departments. Meetings and regular communication showcase the uniqueness of his or her school, its academic outcomes, and the elements of success.

Recommended Reading

Blanchard, Kenneth, and Spencer Johnson. *The One Minute Manager*. New York: Berkley Books, 1982.

Bossidy, Larry, and Ram Charan. *Execution: The Discipline of Getting Things Done*. New York: Crown Business, 2002.

Buckingham, Marcus, and Curt Coffman. *First, Break All The Rules: What the World's Greatest Managers Do Differently*. New York: Simon & Schuster, 1999.

Carpenter, Brian L. *Charter School Board University*, second edition. The National Charter School Institute, March 1, 2009.

Dourado, Phil. *The 60 Second Leader*. New York: Capstone, 2007.

Pink, Daniel H. *Drive: The Surprising Truth About What Motivates Us*. New York: Riverhead Books, 2009.

Pomerance Brick, Wendi. *The Science of Service: Six Essential Elements for Creating a Culture of Service*. Escondido, CA: CoCo Publishing, 2010.

Welch, Jack. *Jack: Straight From The Gut*. With John A. Byrne. New York: Warner Books, 2001.

Wilke, Steve, and Rebecca Wilke. *Corporate Family Matters: Creating and Developing Organizational Dynasties*. San Diego: LEADon, 2010.

About the Author

Cameron Curry has an extensive background in business development prior to helping found The Classical Academy K–8 charter school in 1999.

In 2003 he co-founded the K–8 public charter school Coastal Academy, and in 2006, Classical Academy High School. His entrepreneurial spirit and experience has been a great benefit to the operation of these schools.

Under his leadership, the schools have received the Exemplary Recognition Award from the California Department of Education and California Consortium for Independent Study for high-quality programming. They were the first three charter schools in California to hold this recognition.

In alignment with embracing quality, Coastal Academy was named a California Distinguished School in 2010. In 2011, he established the first Personalized Learning Center to augment and expand K–12 grade options for The Classical Academies.

Cameron is also a strong advocate for school choice and provides ongoing support to charter school developers with questions, resources, and information on exemplary independent study operations and programming.

In 2011, Cameron received the Hart Vision Award from the California Charter Schools Association as its Charter School Leader of the Year.

Made in the USA
Columbia, SC
13 January 2018